My first BIG BOOK of COLORING

By
Berhane Mustapha

This Book Belongs To

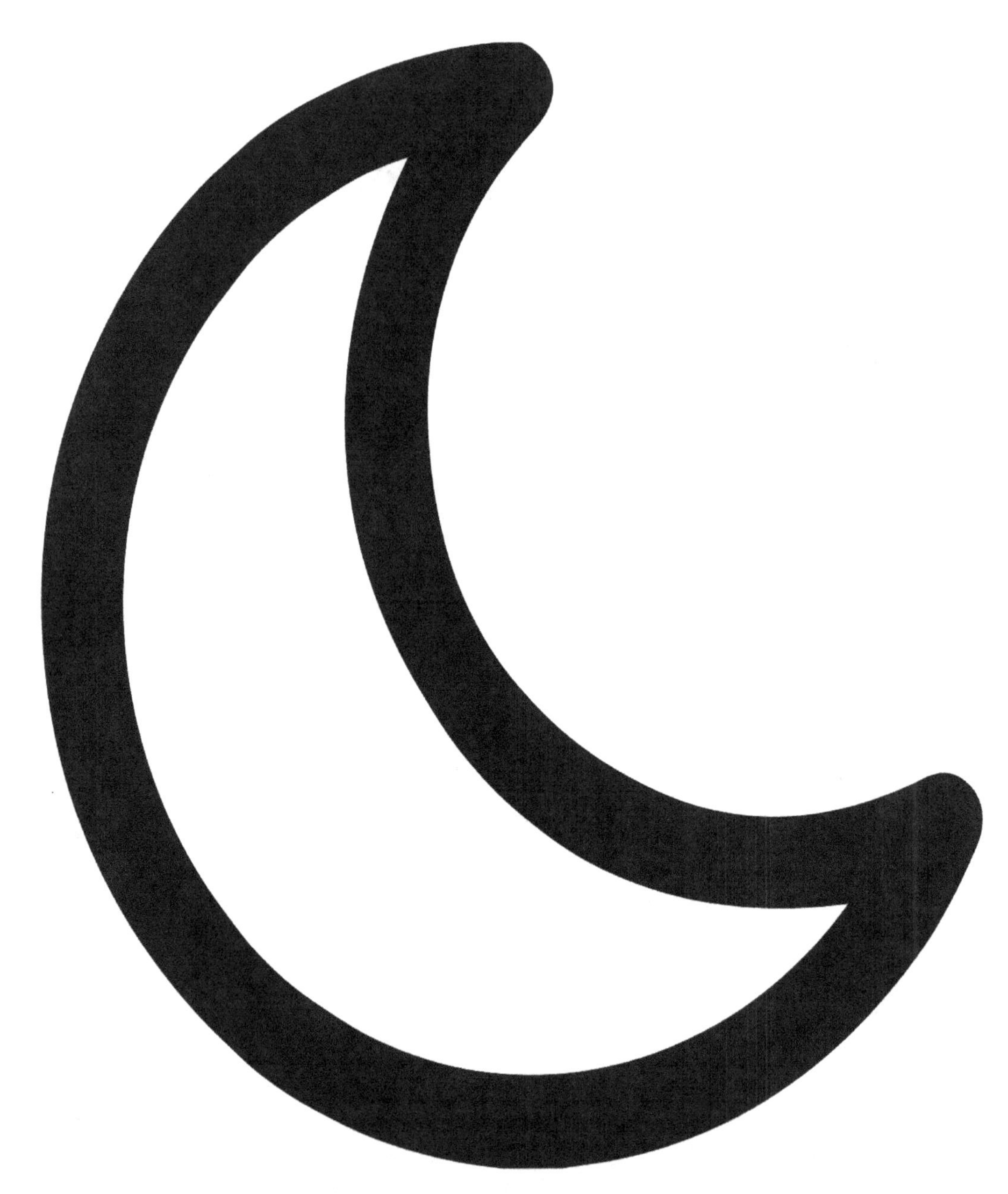

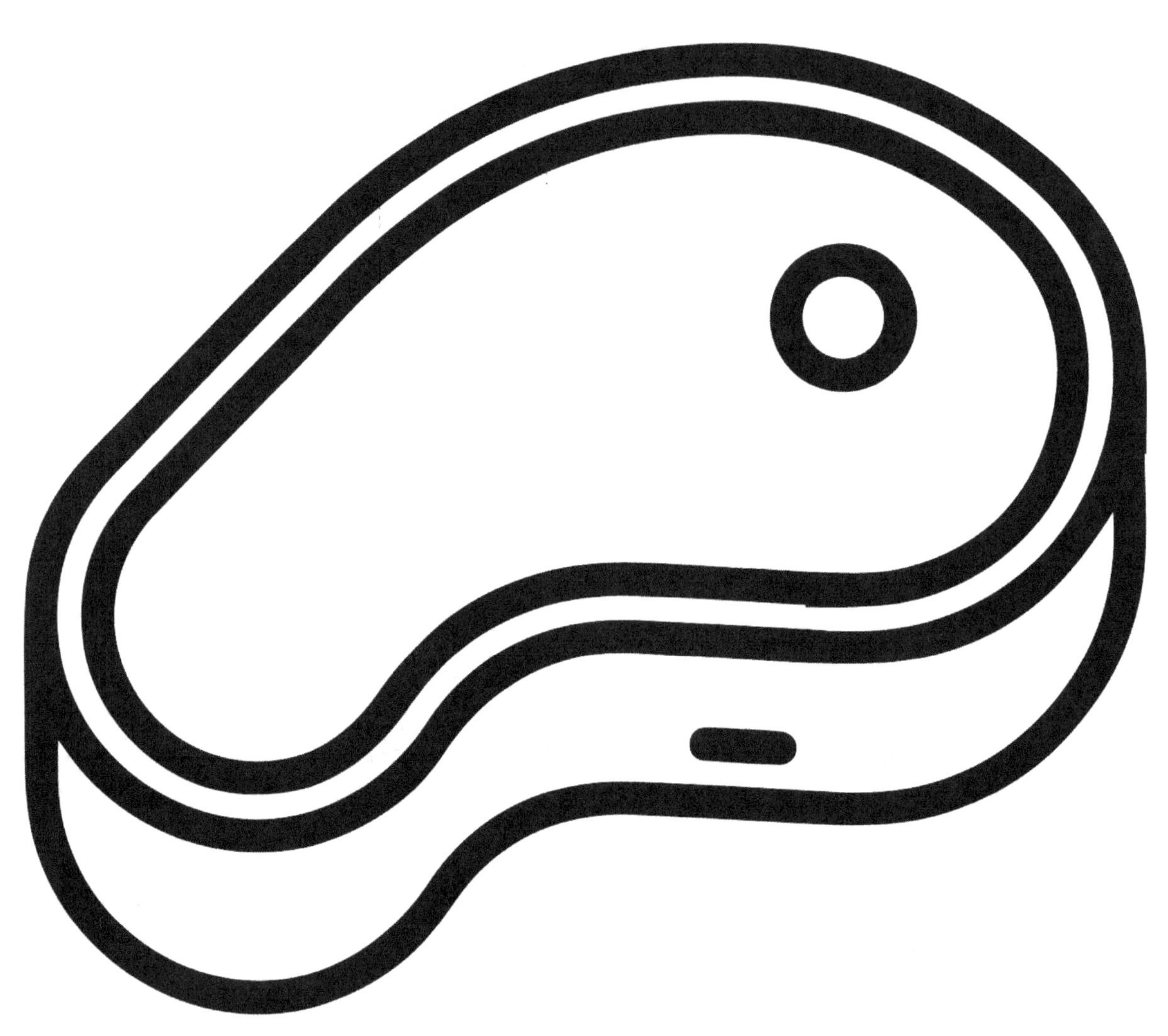

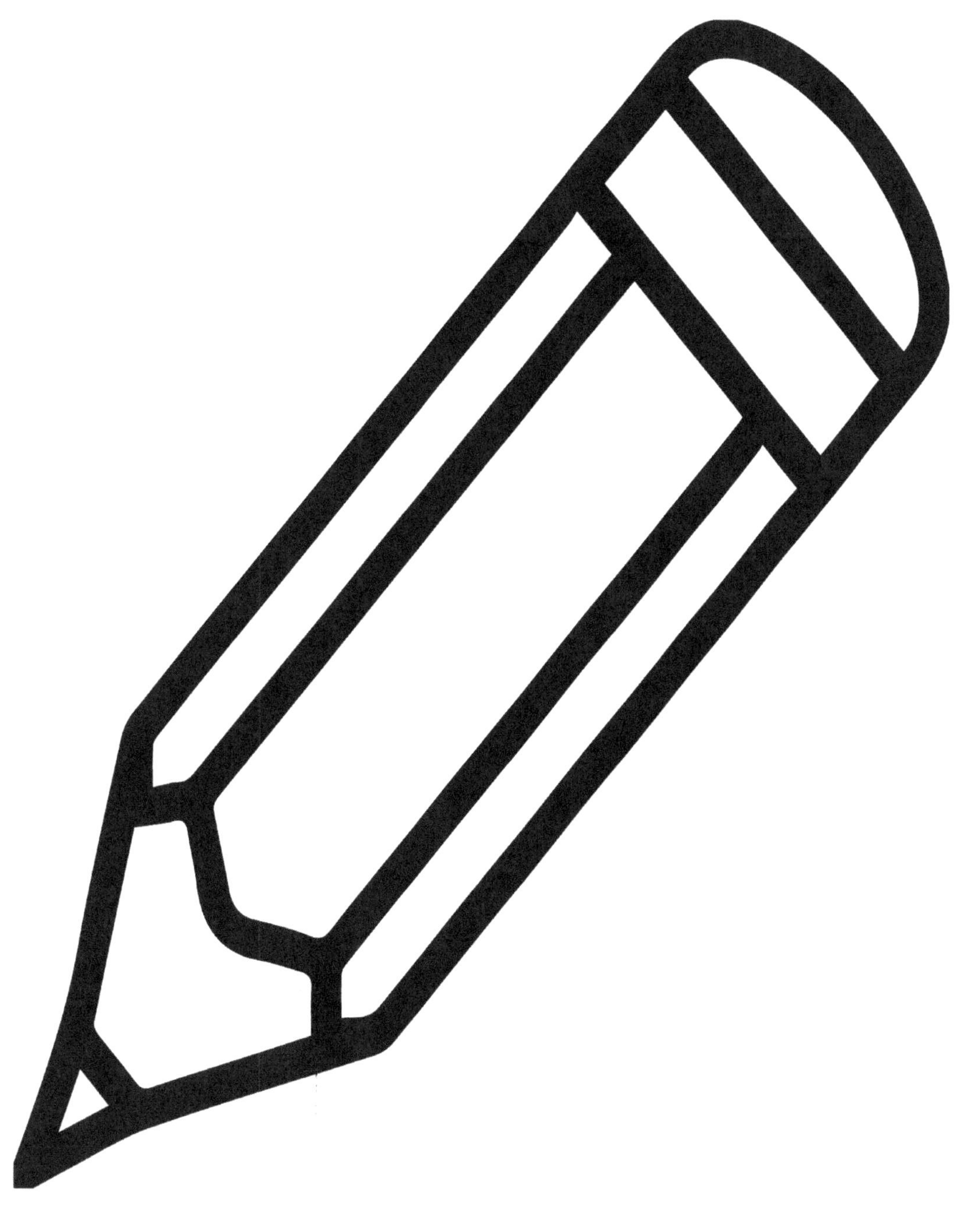

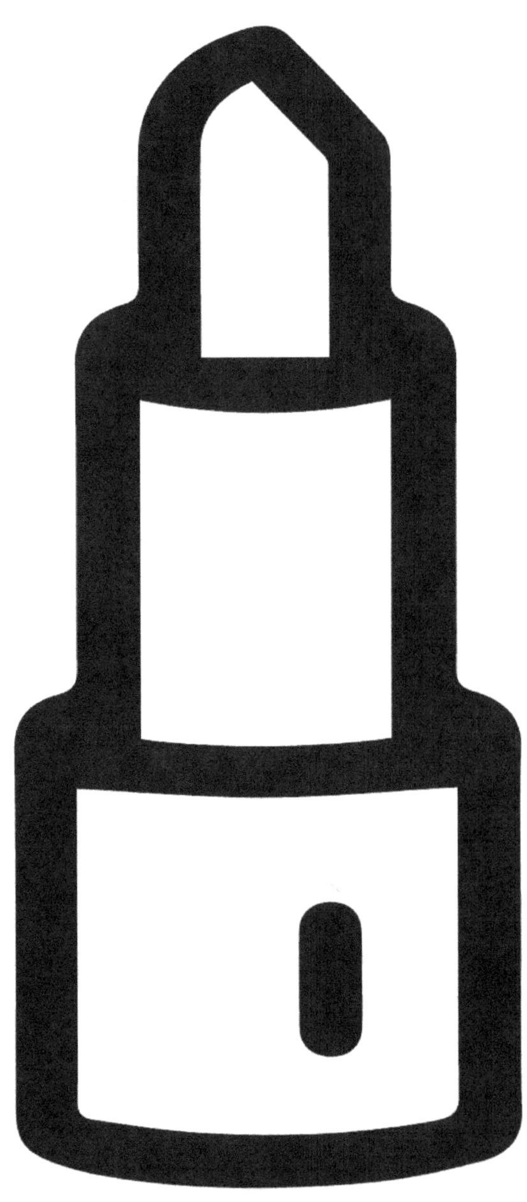

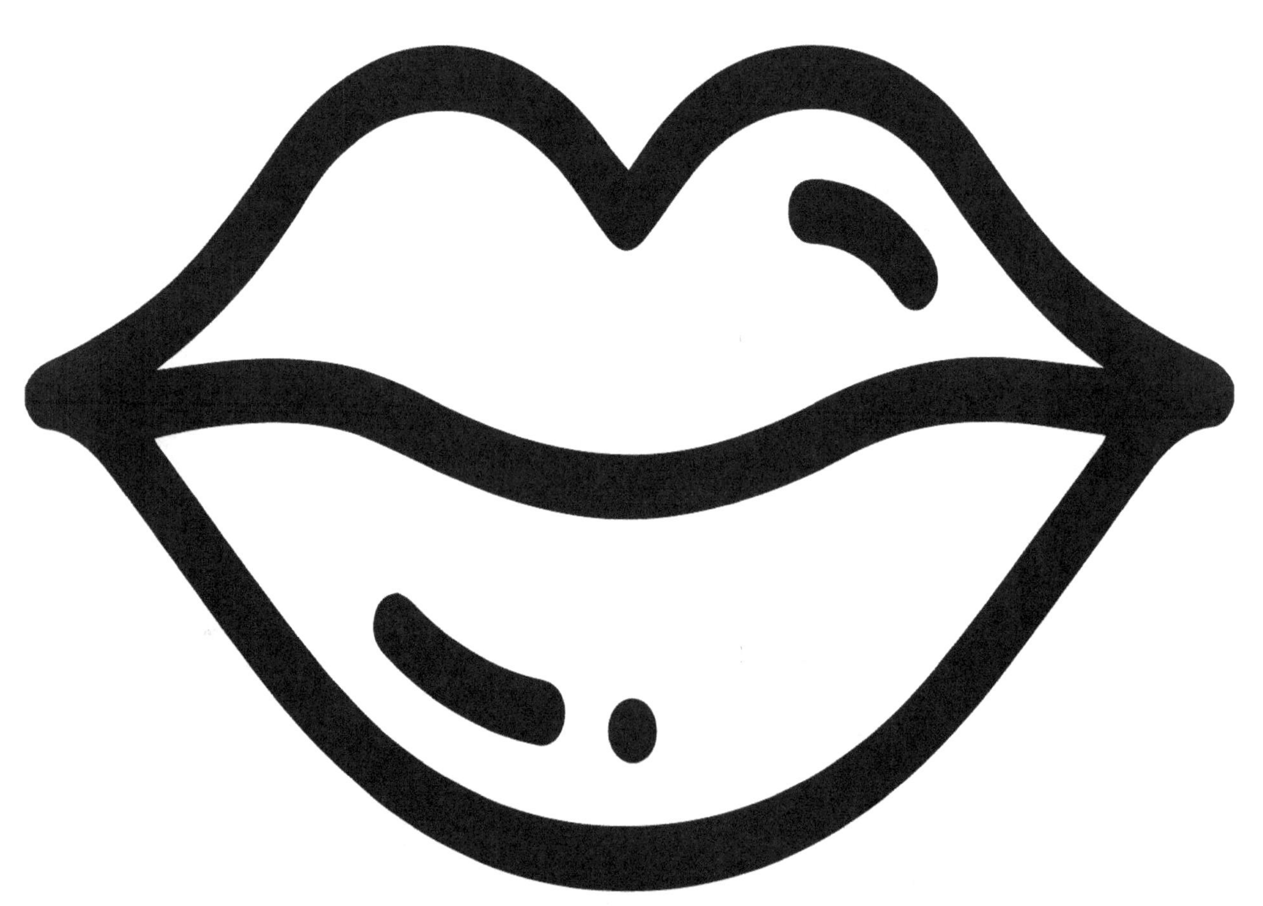

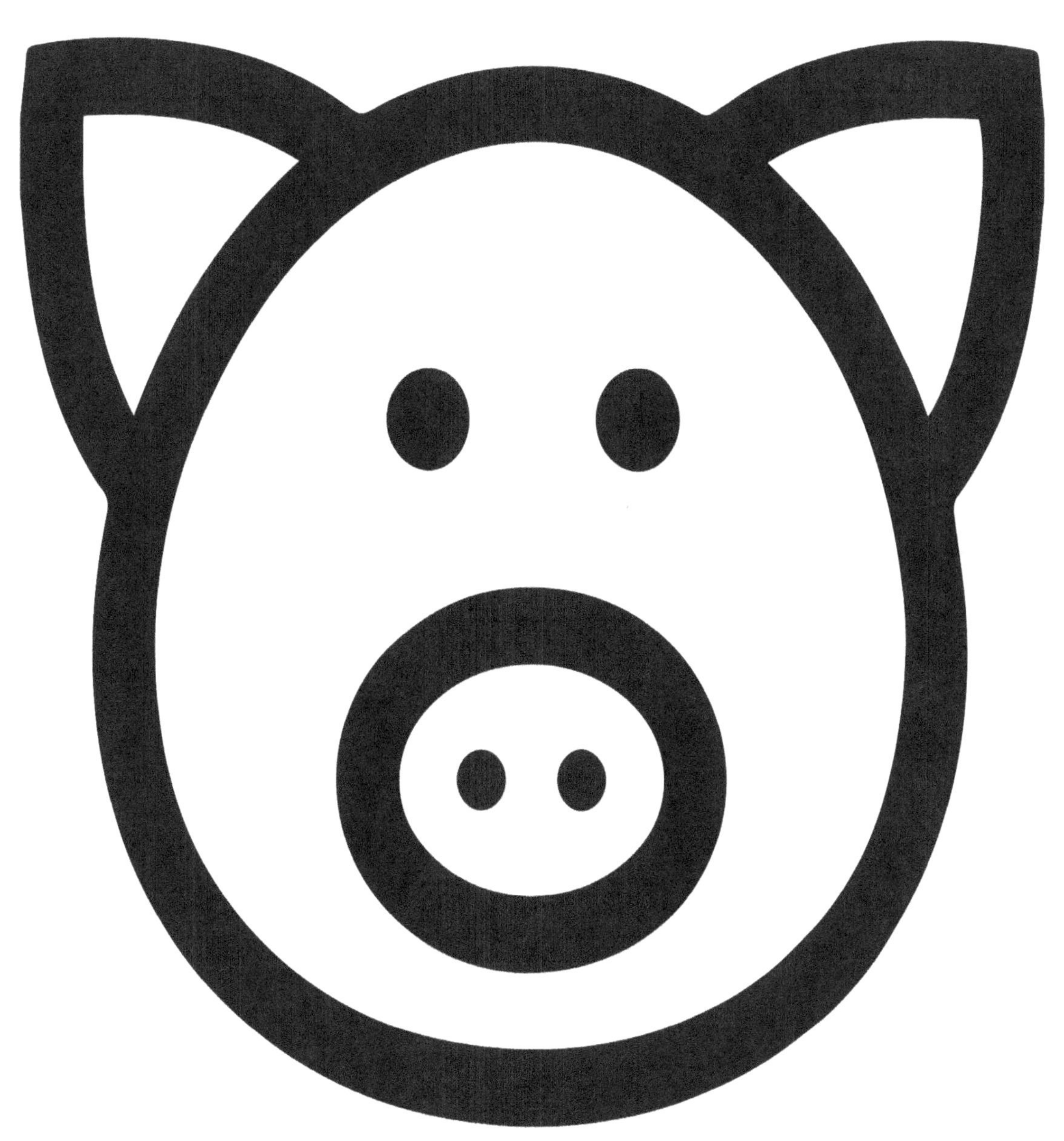

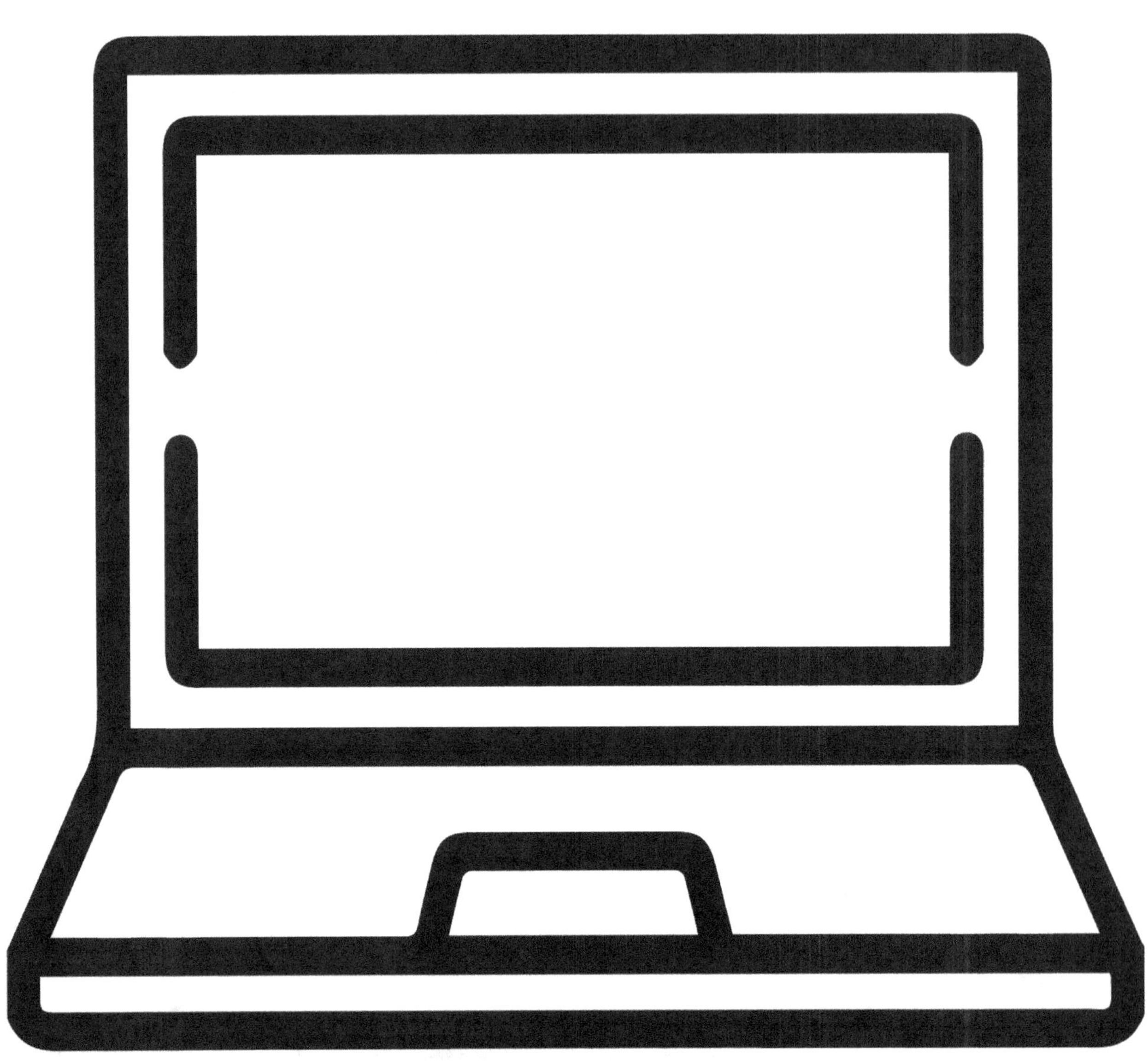

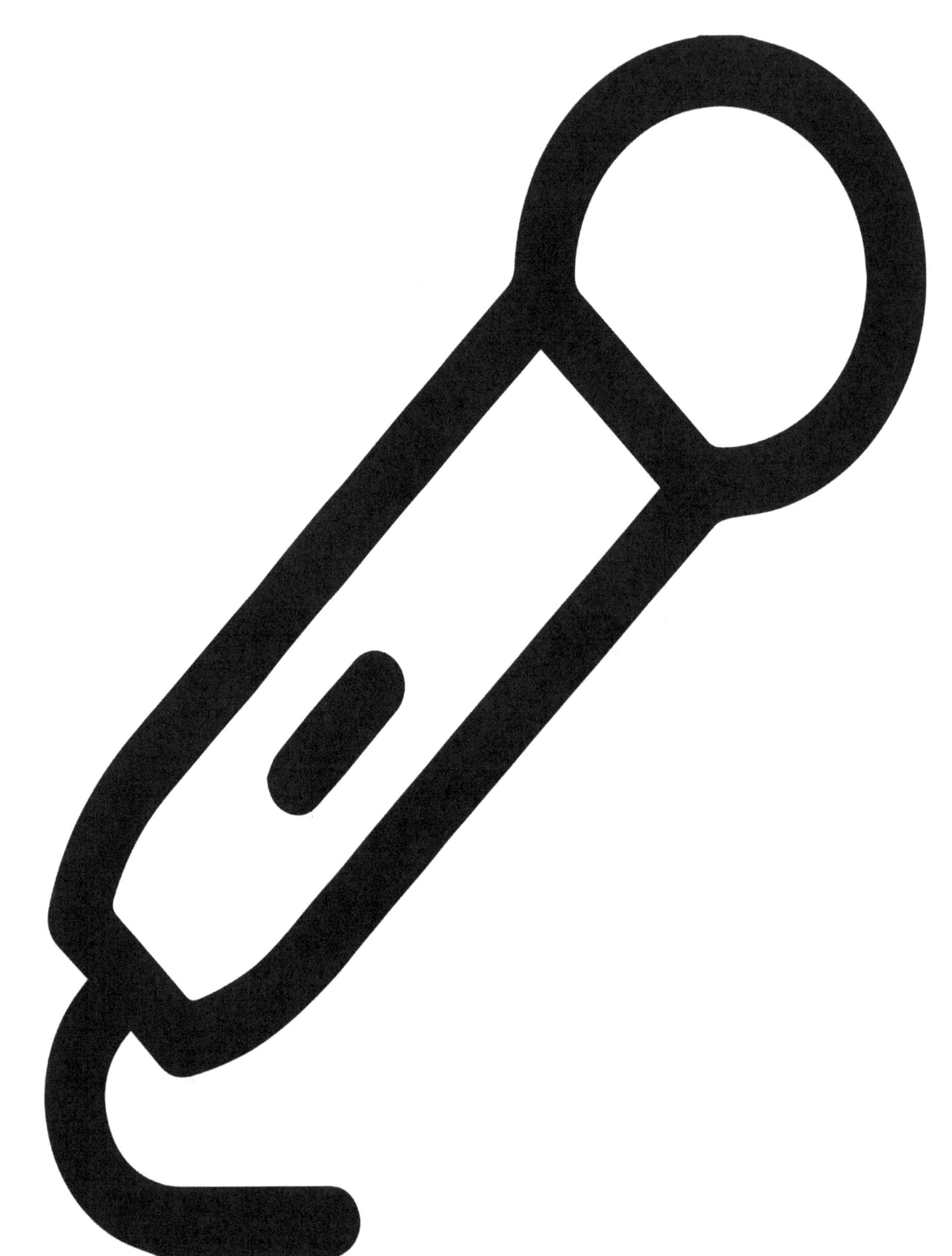

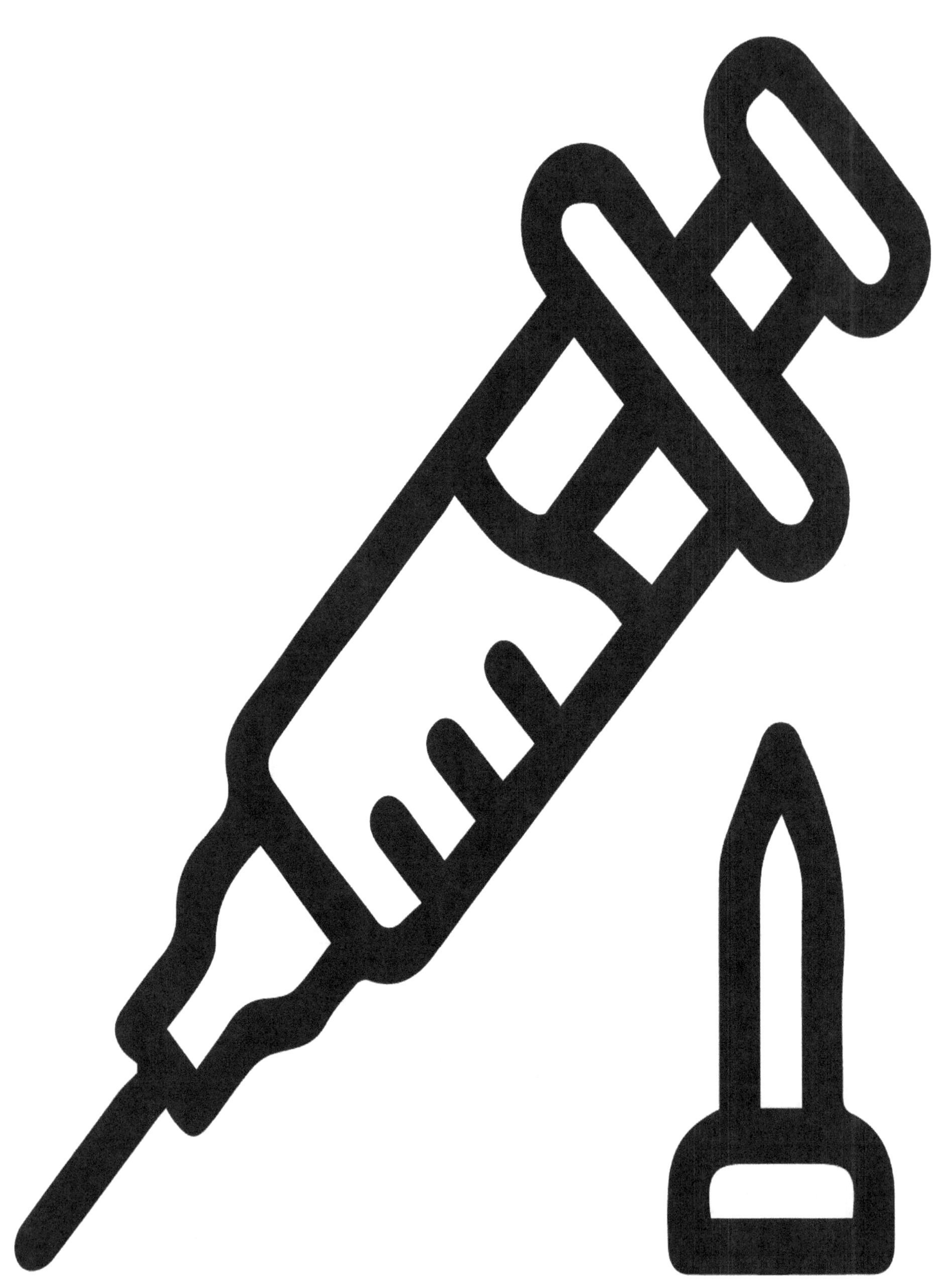

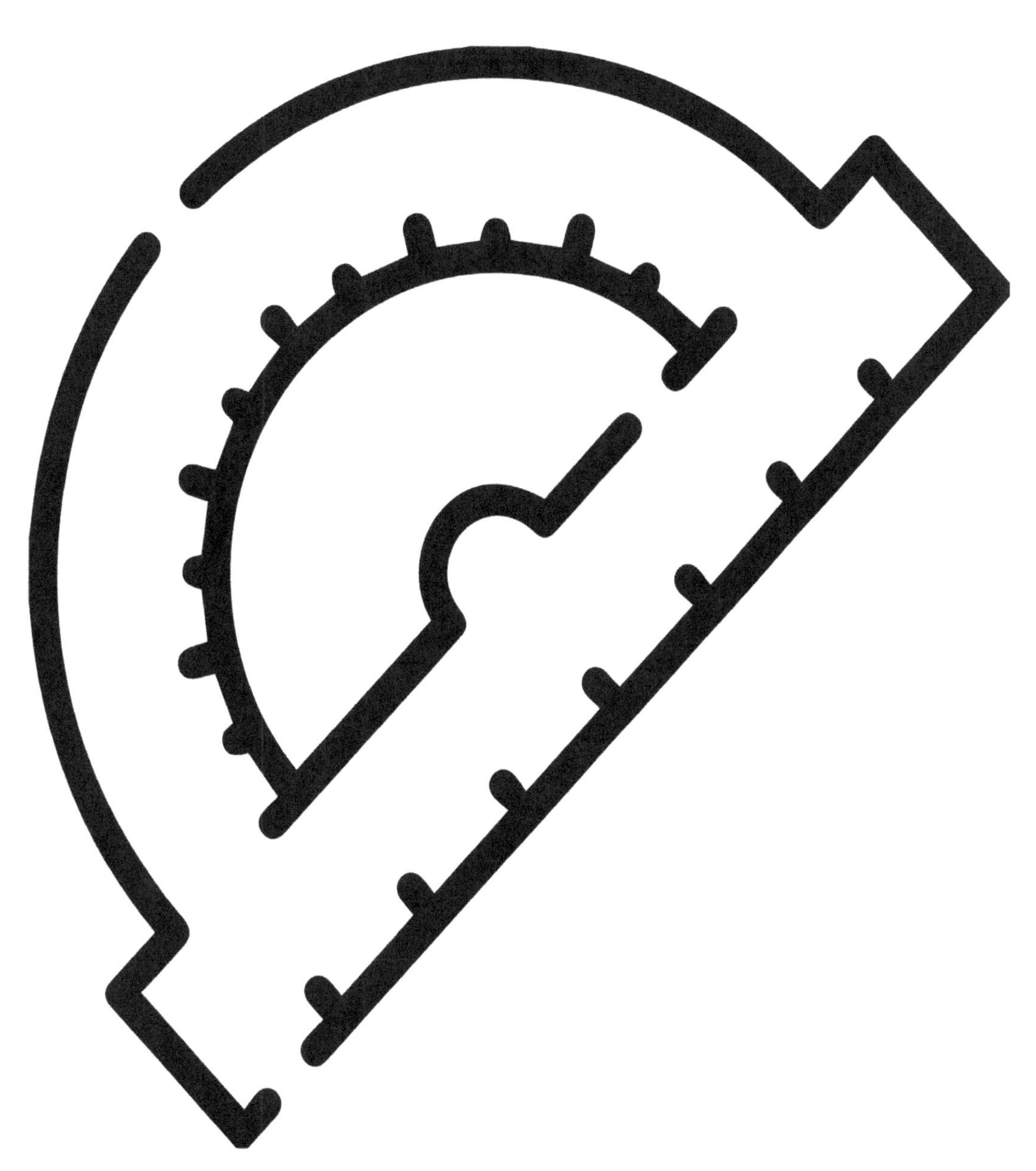

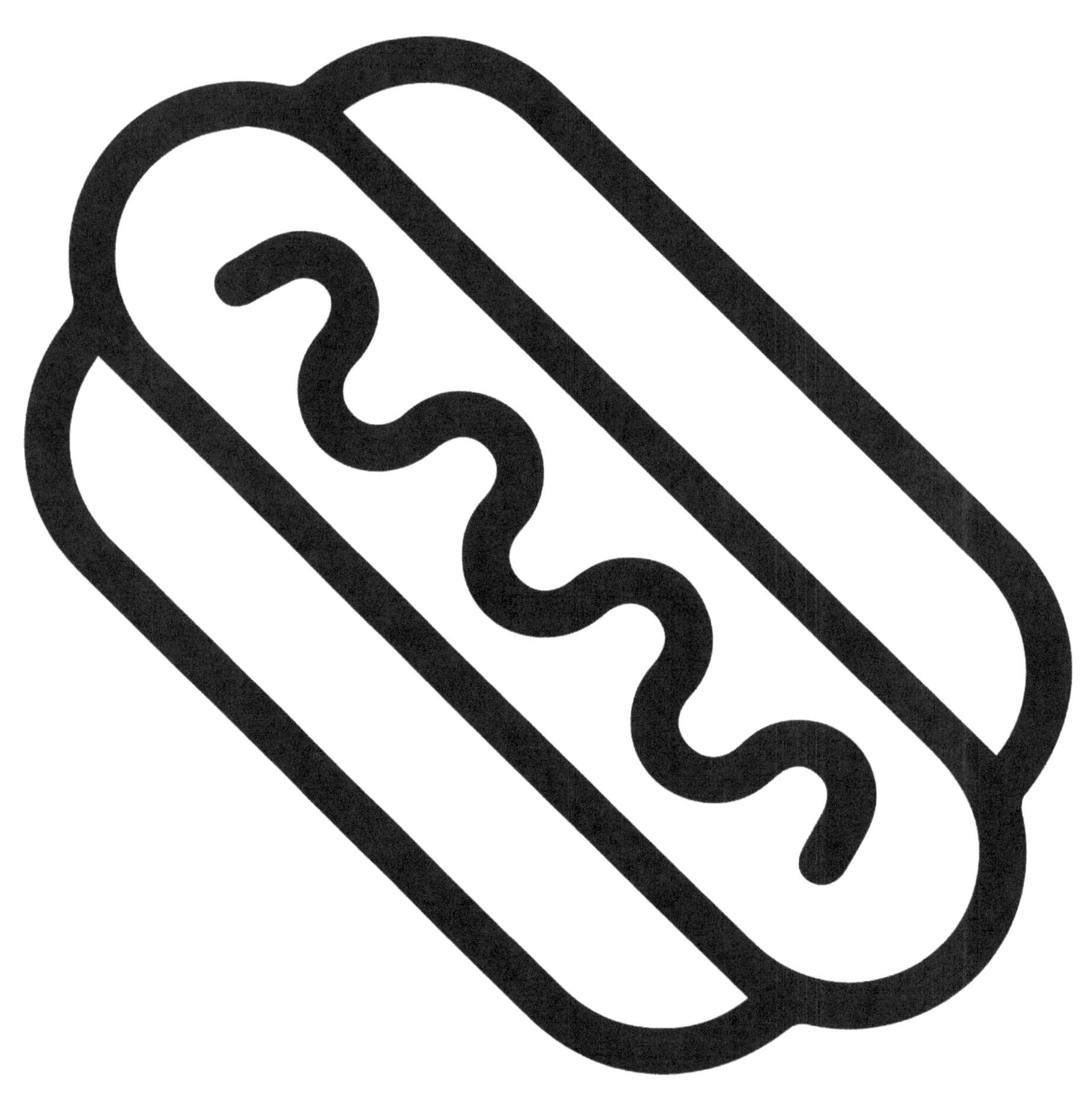

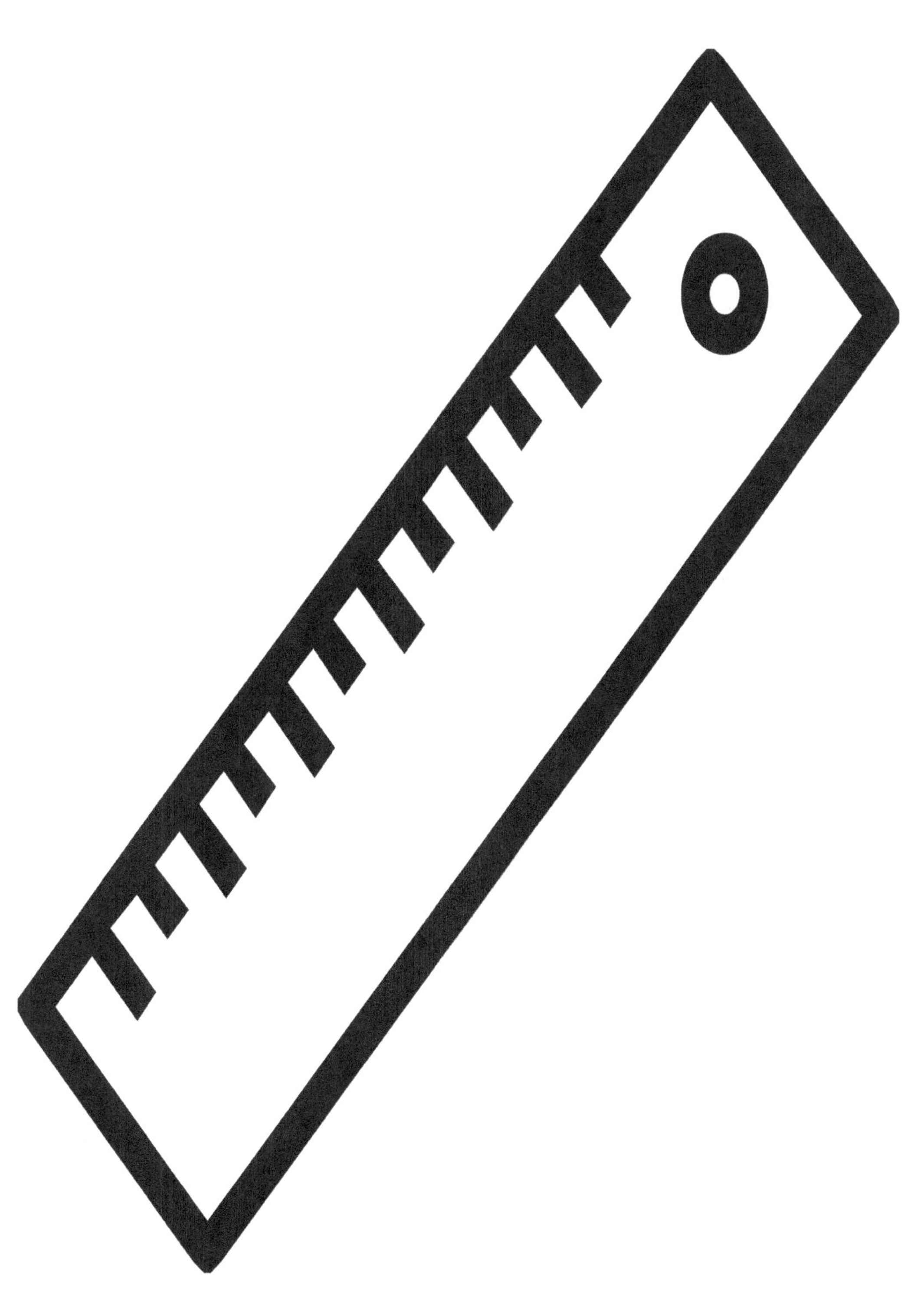

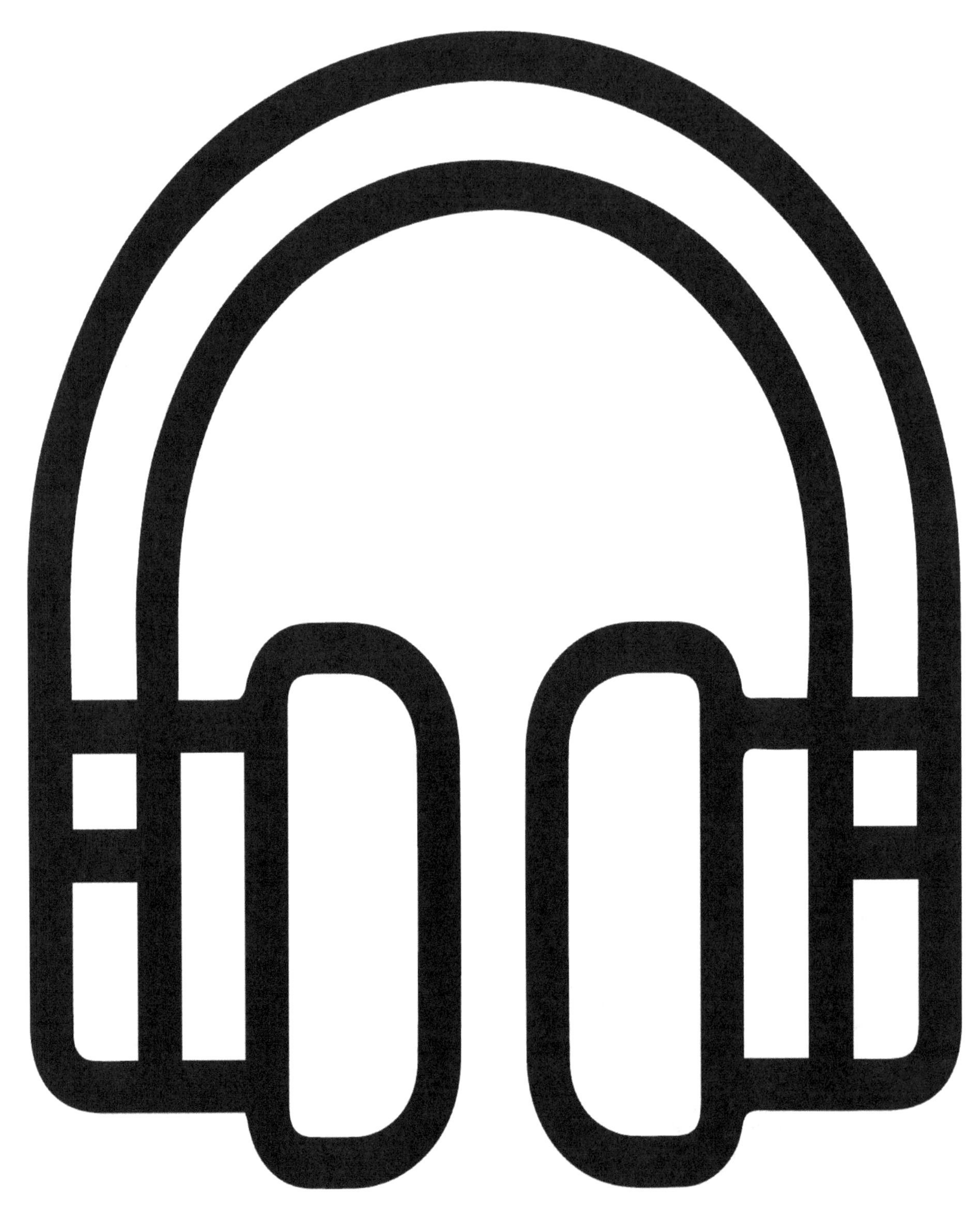

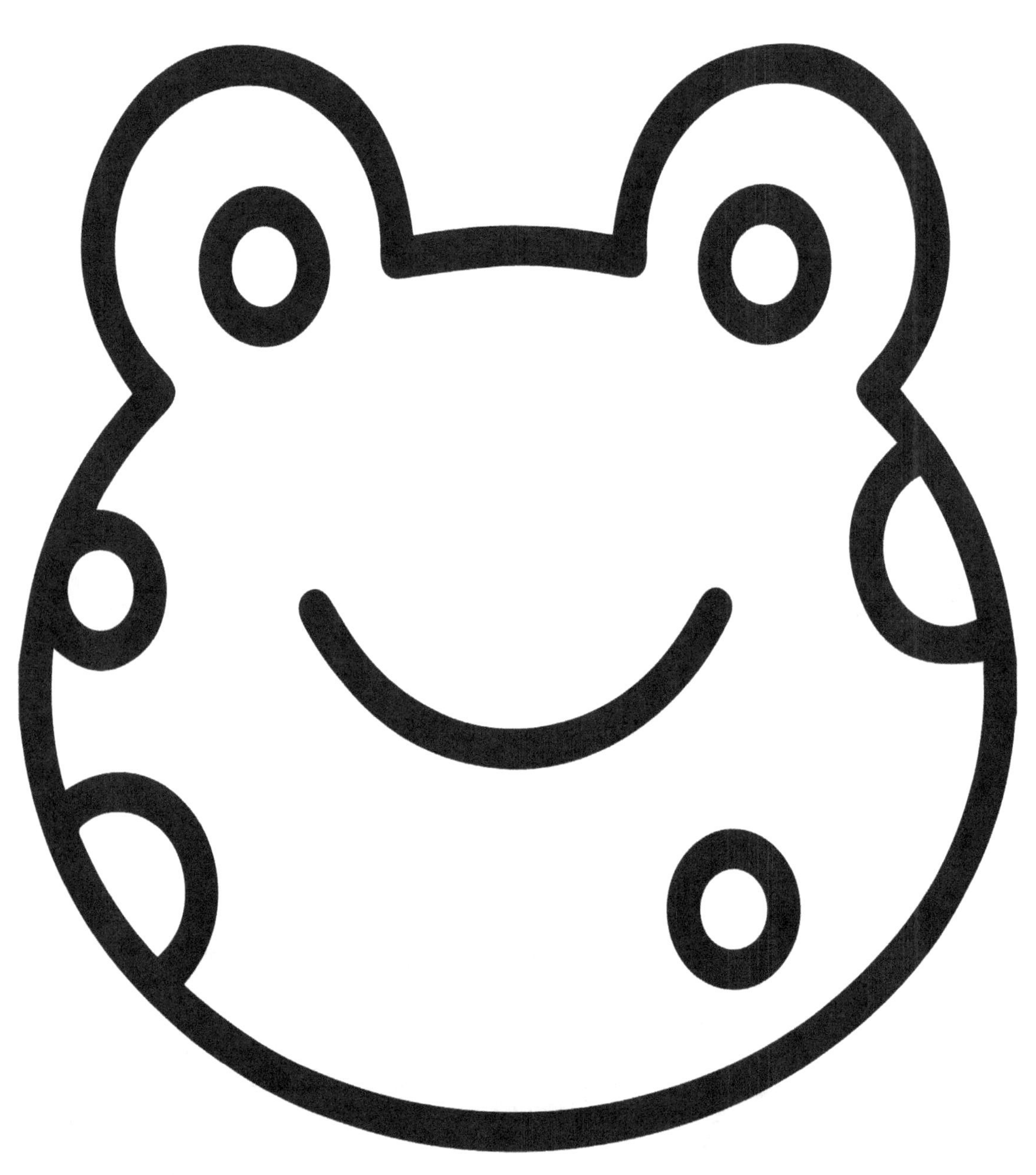

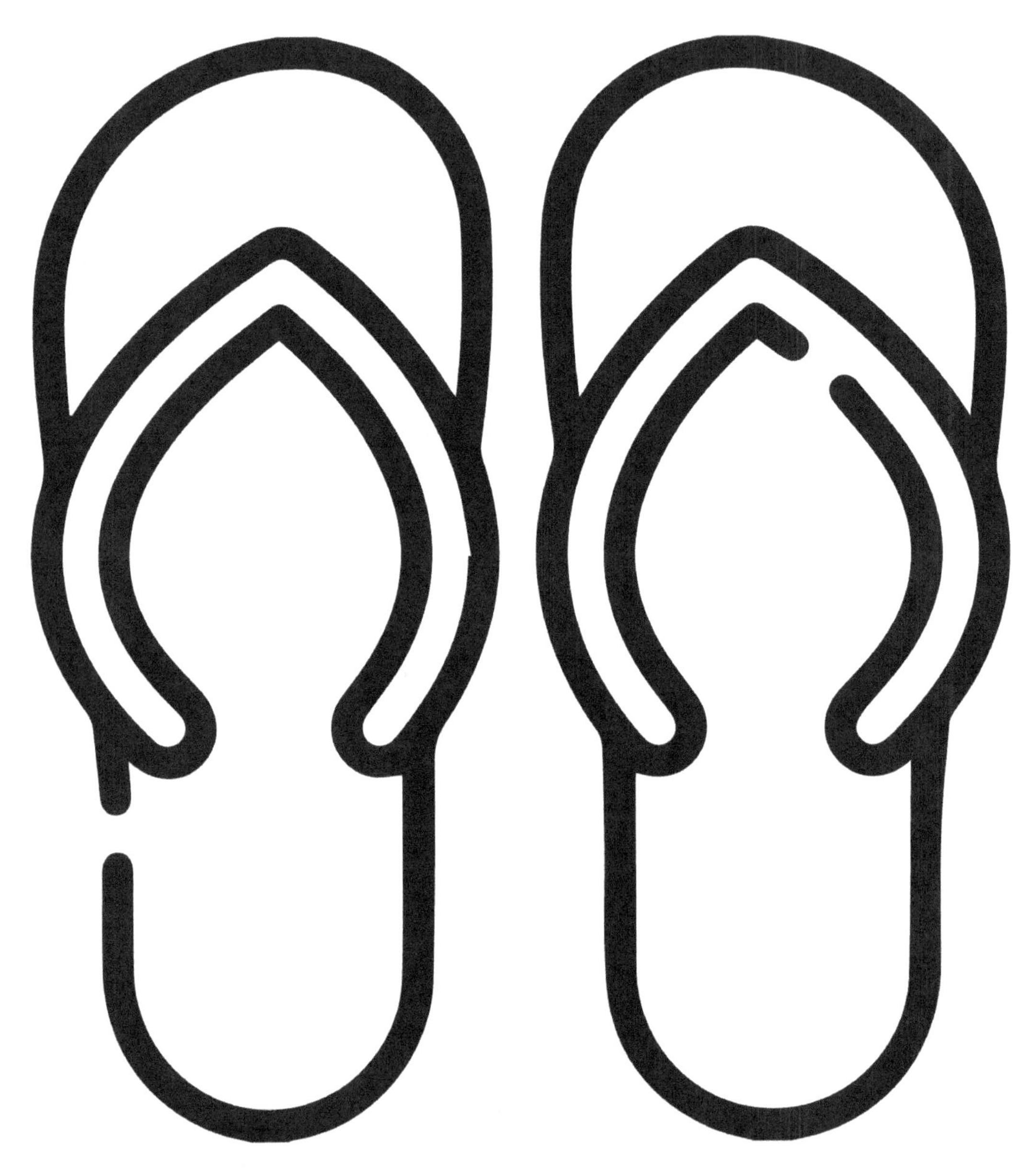

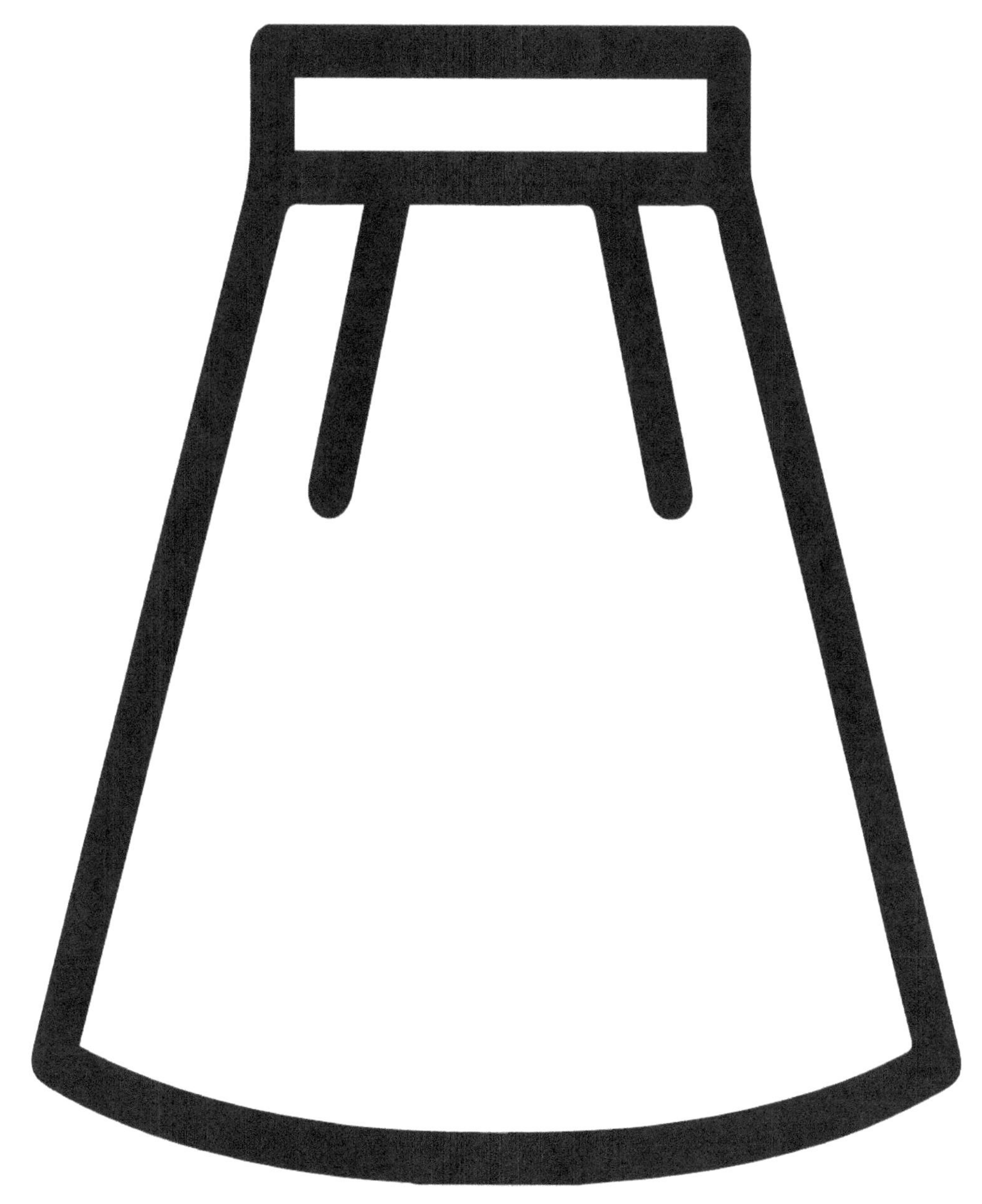

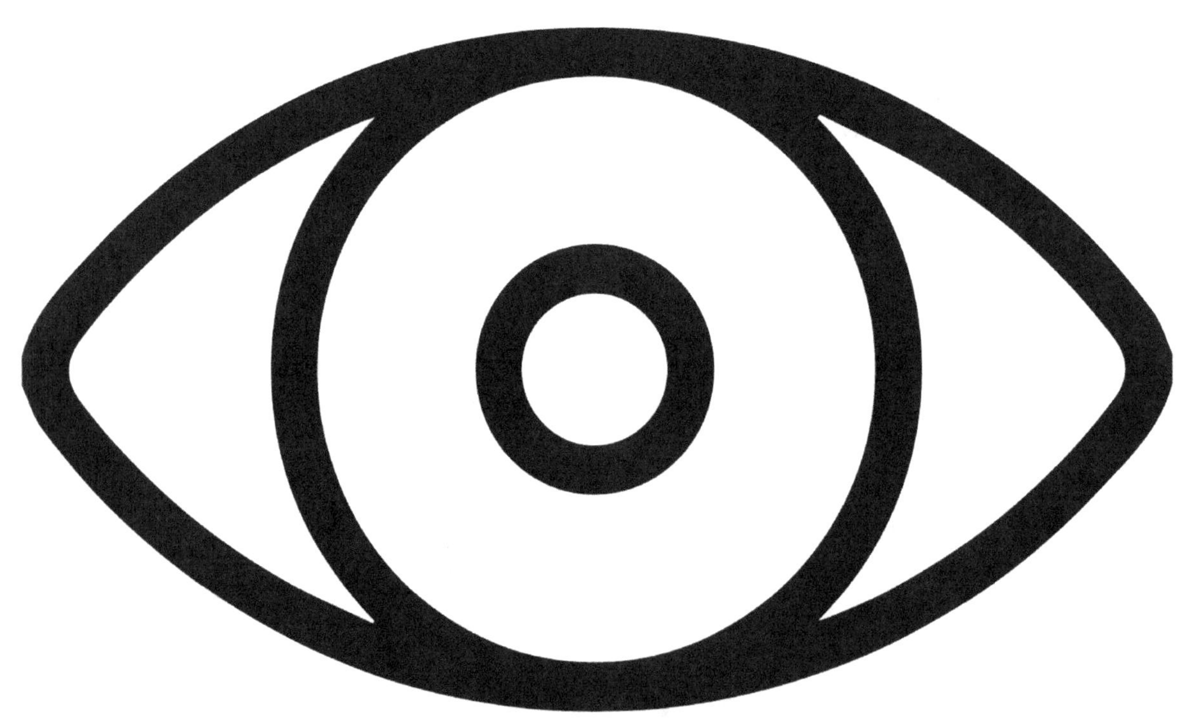

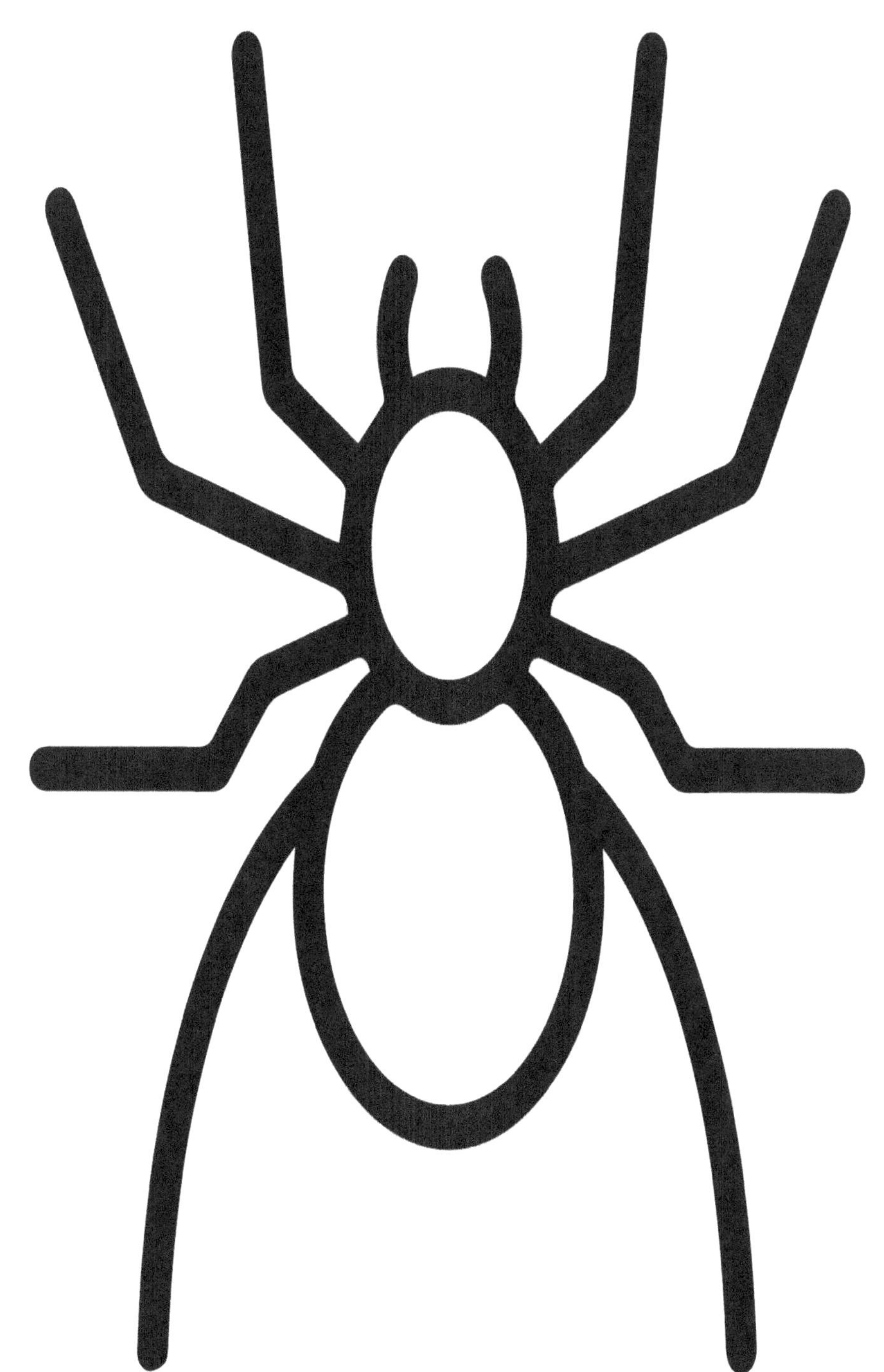

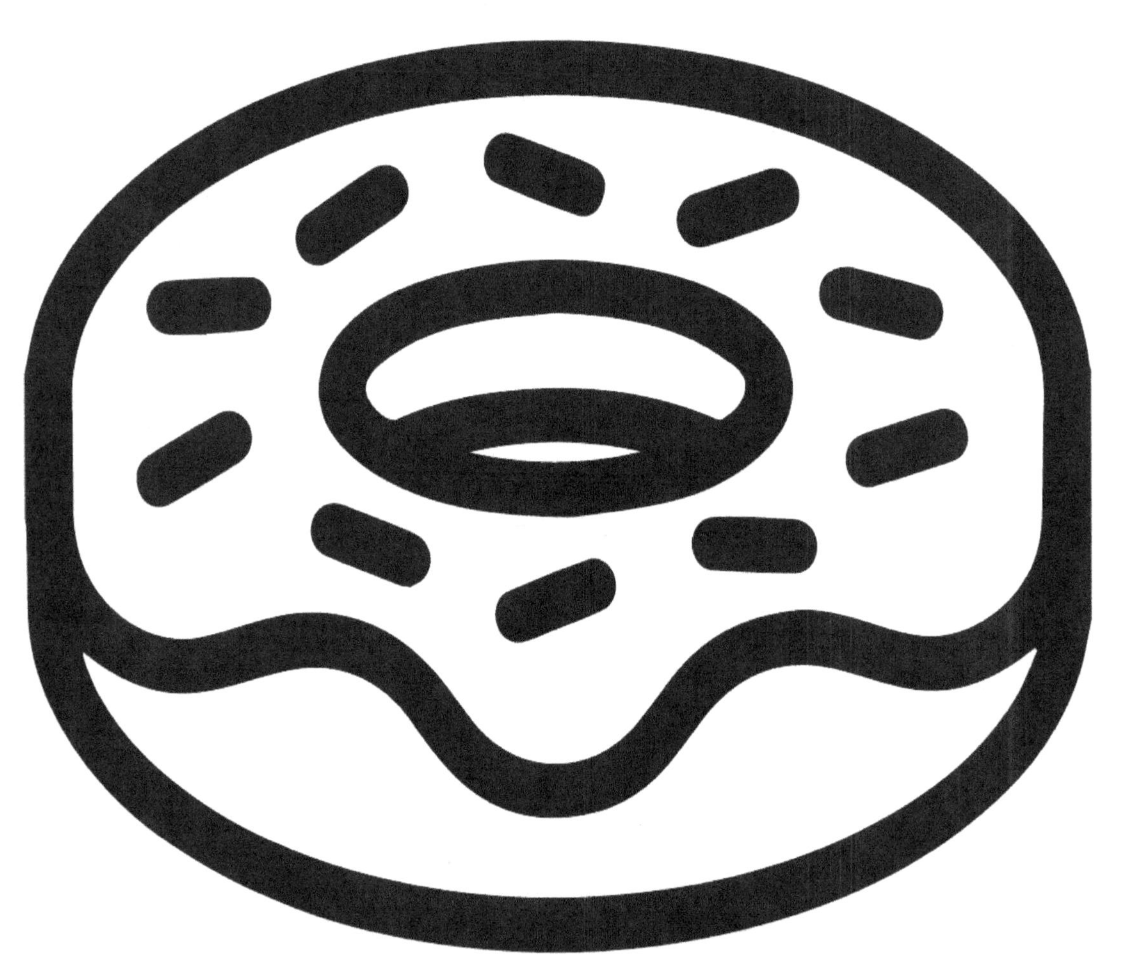

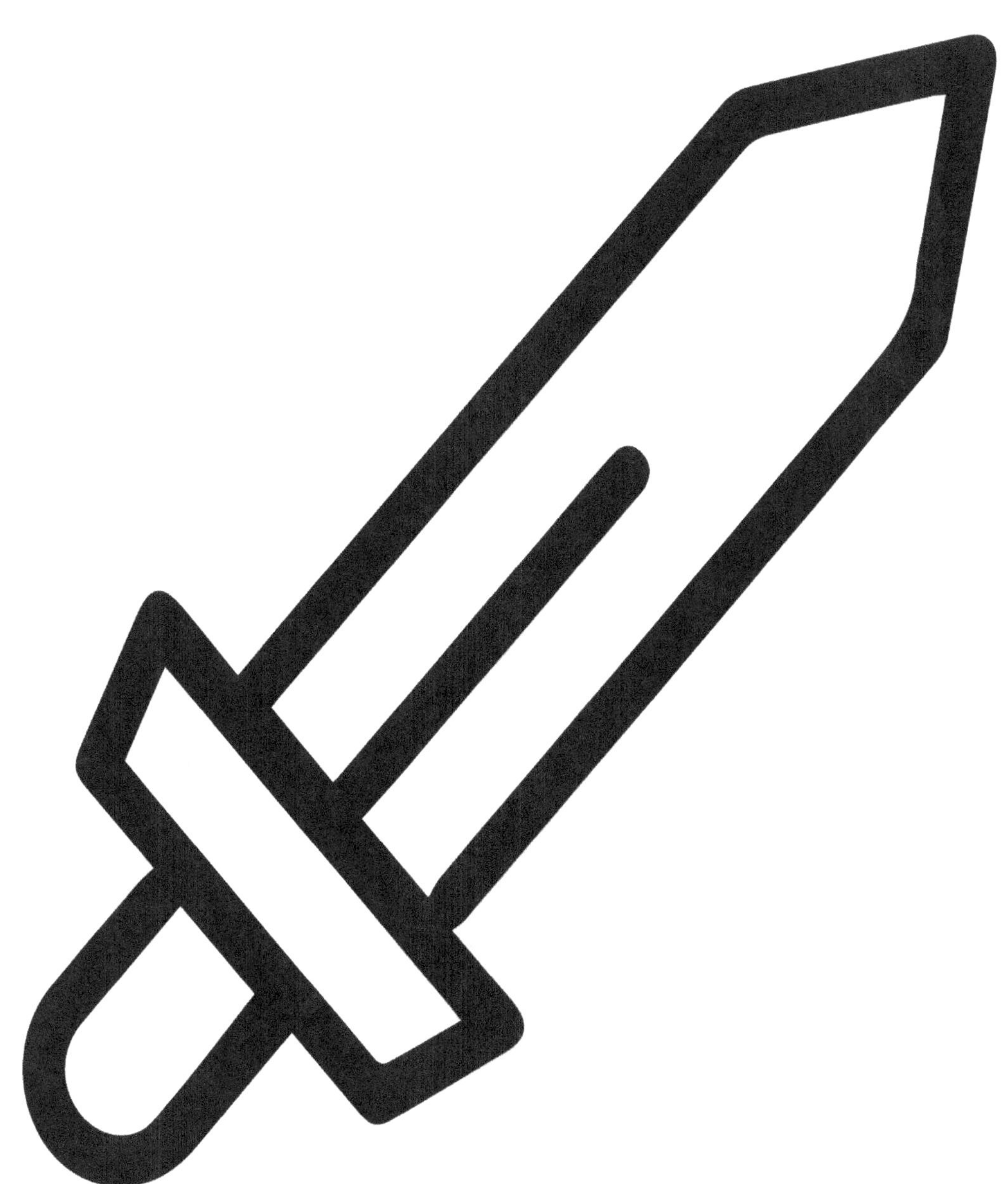

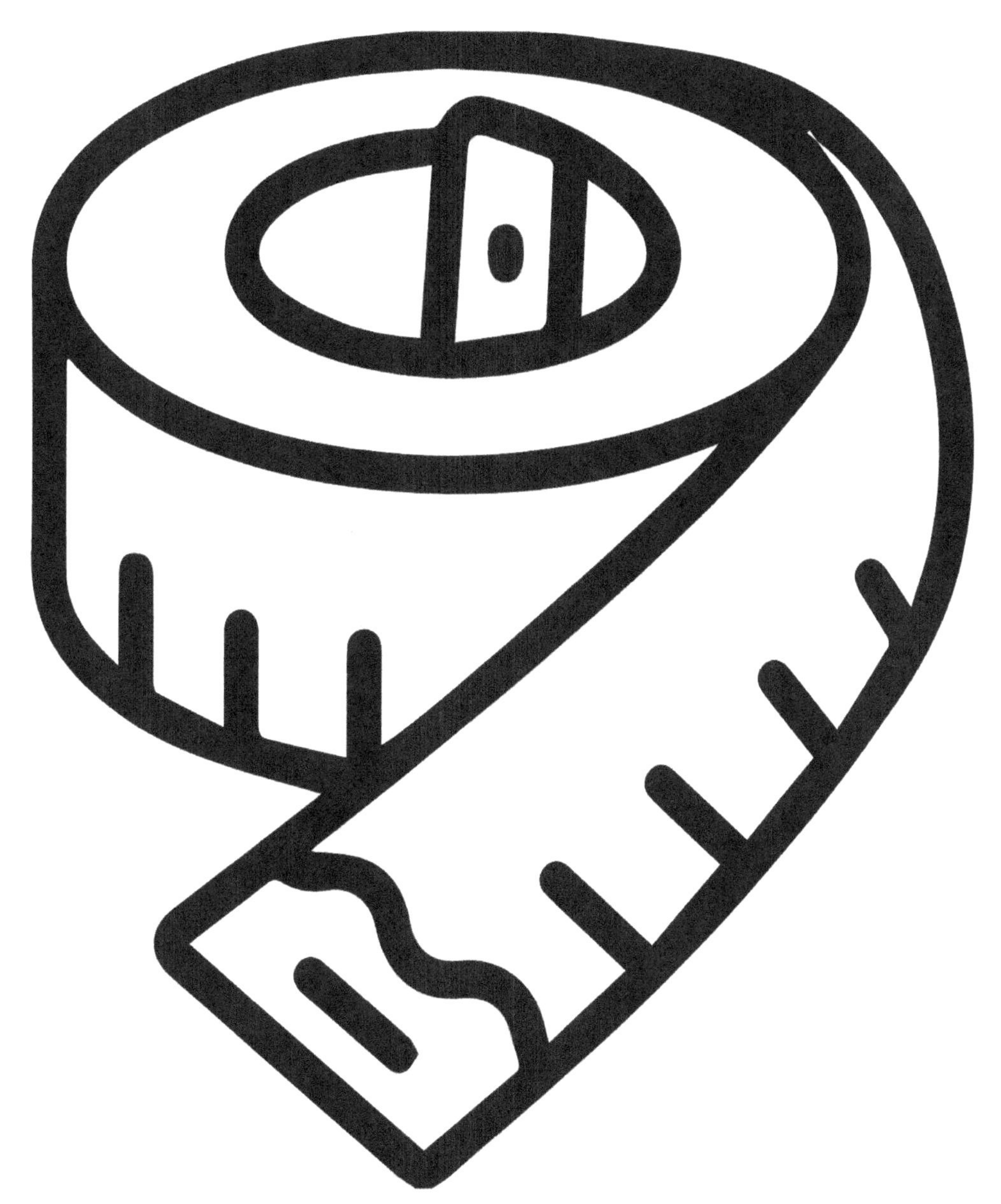

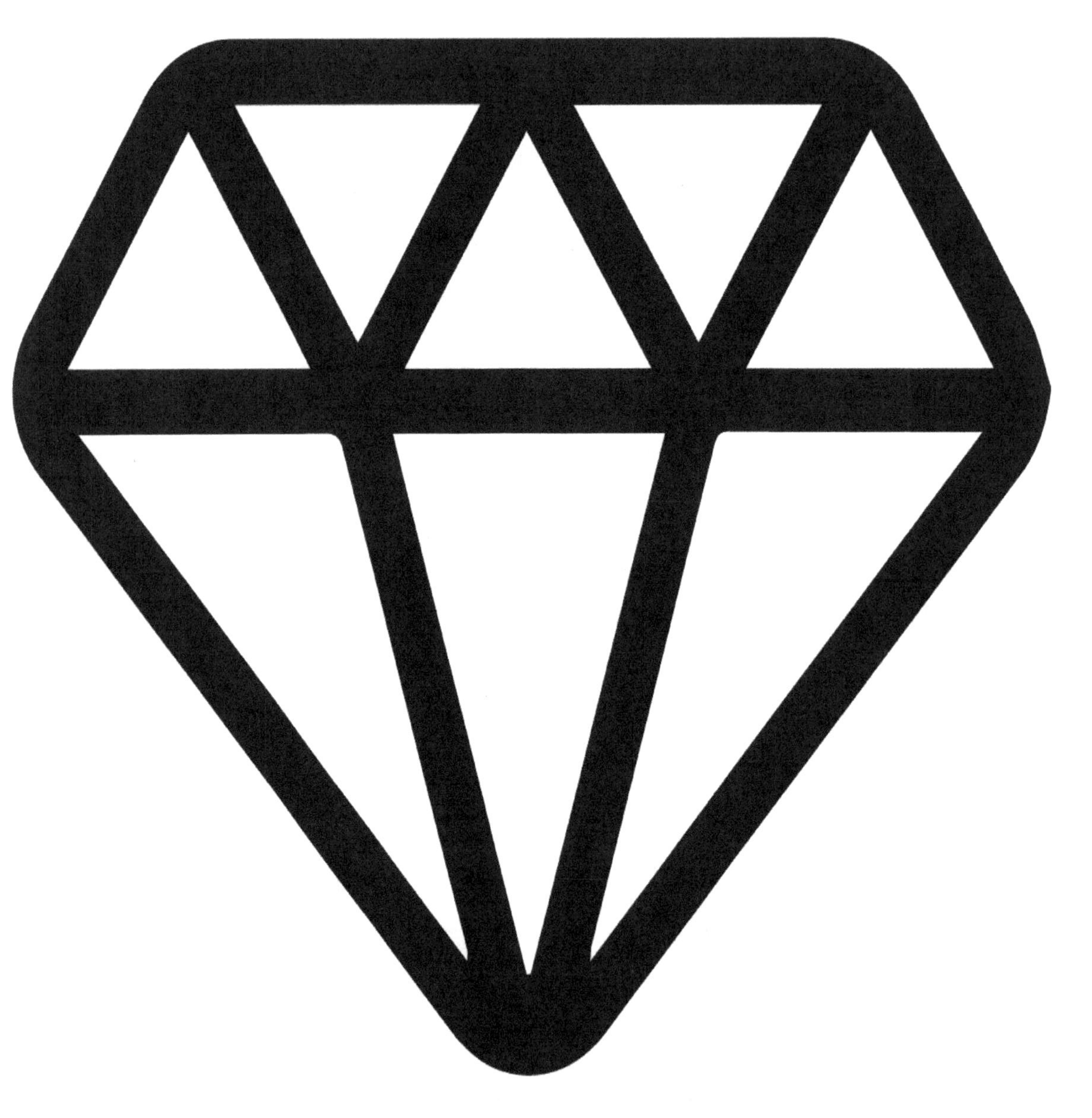

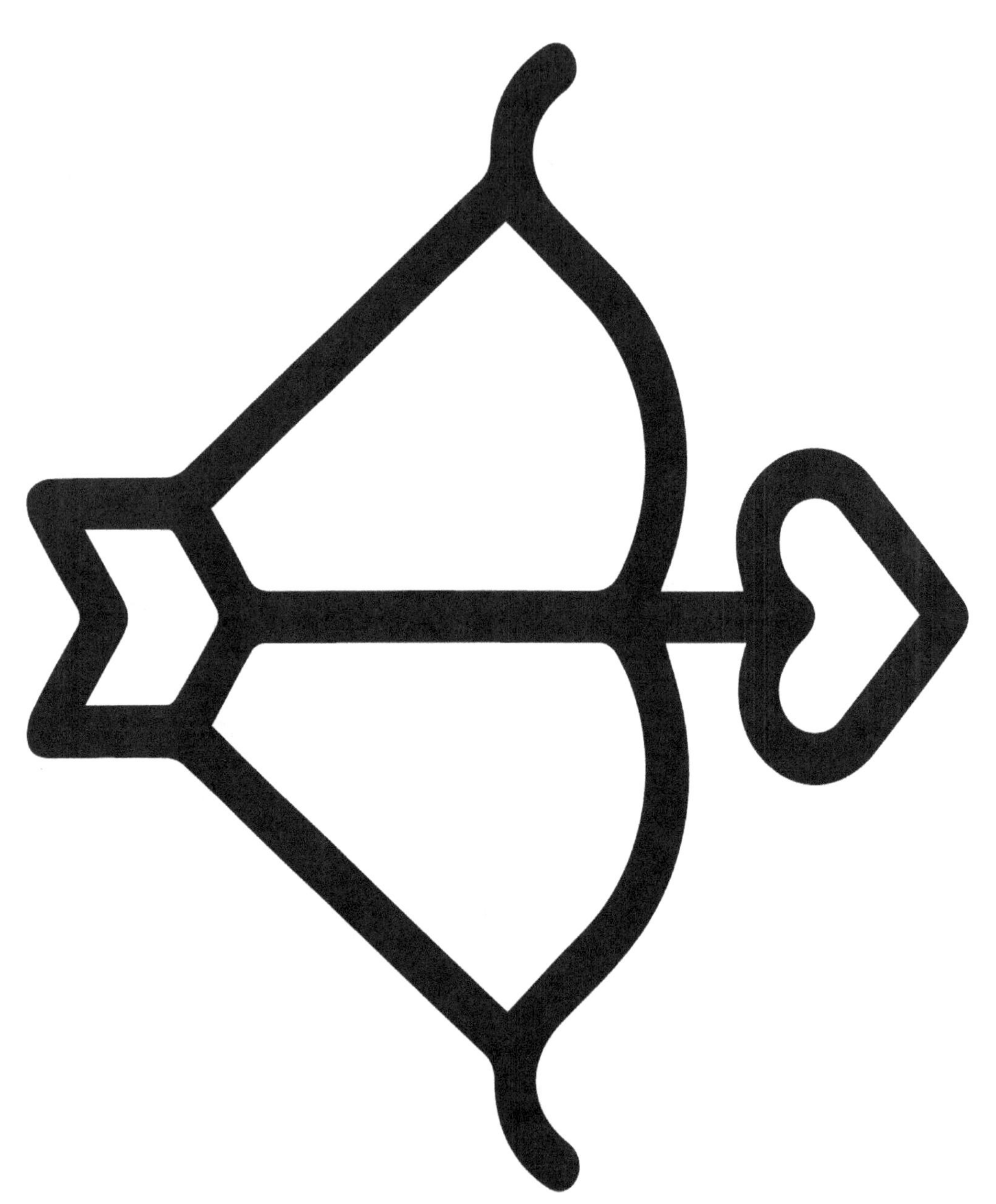

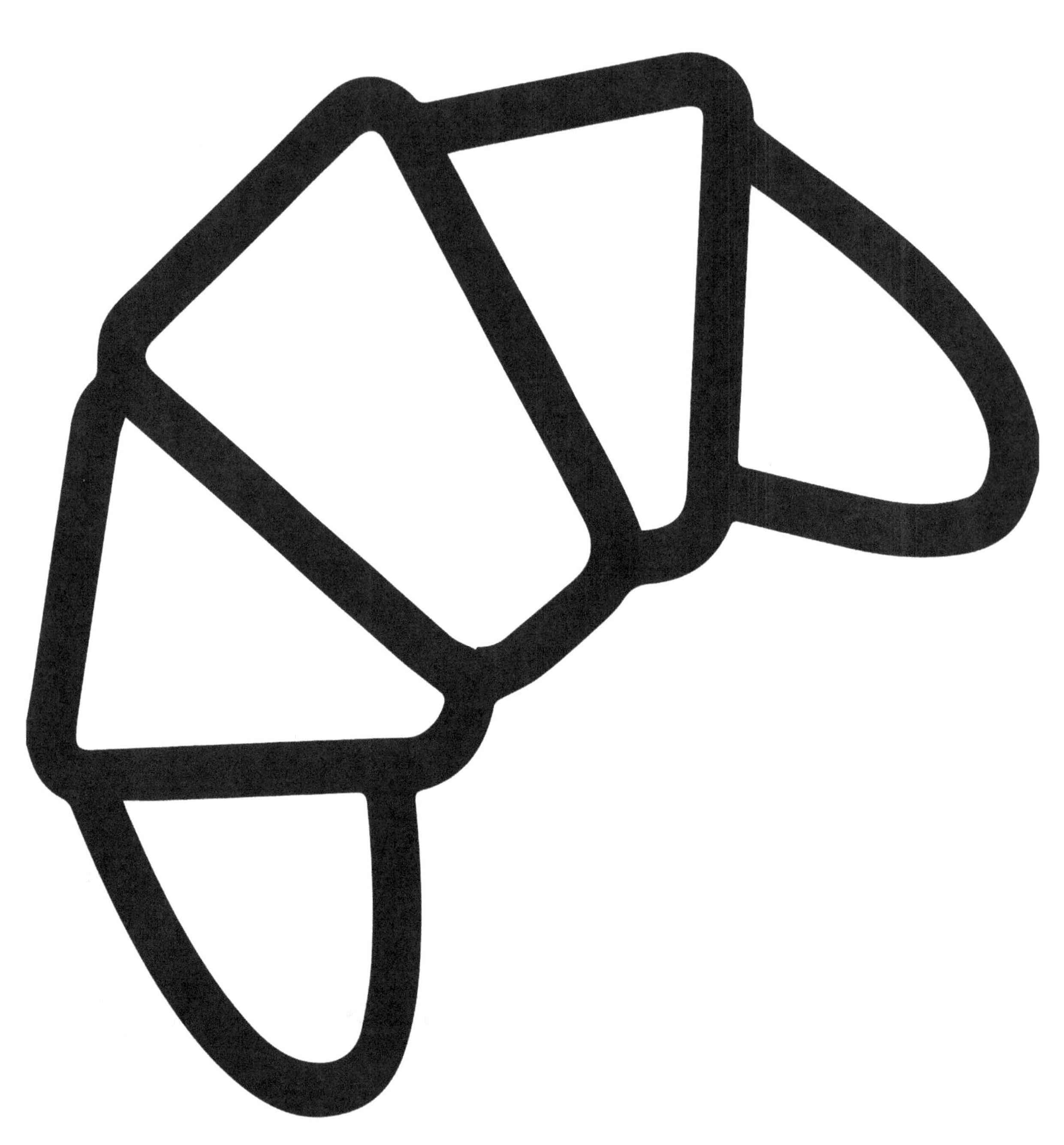

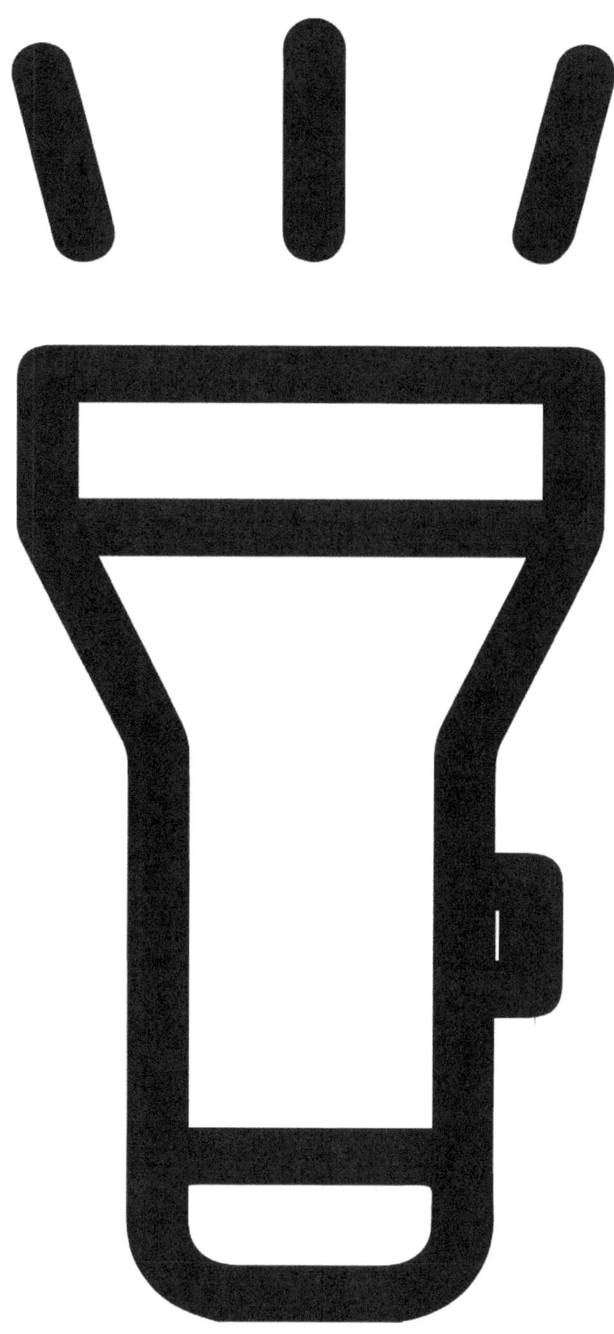

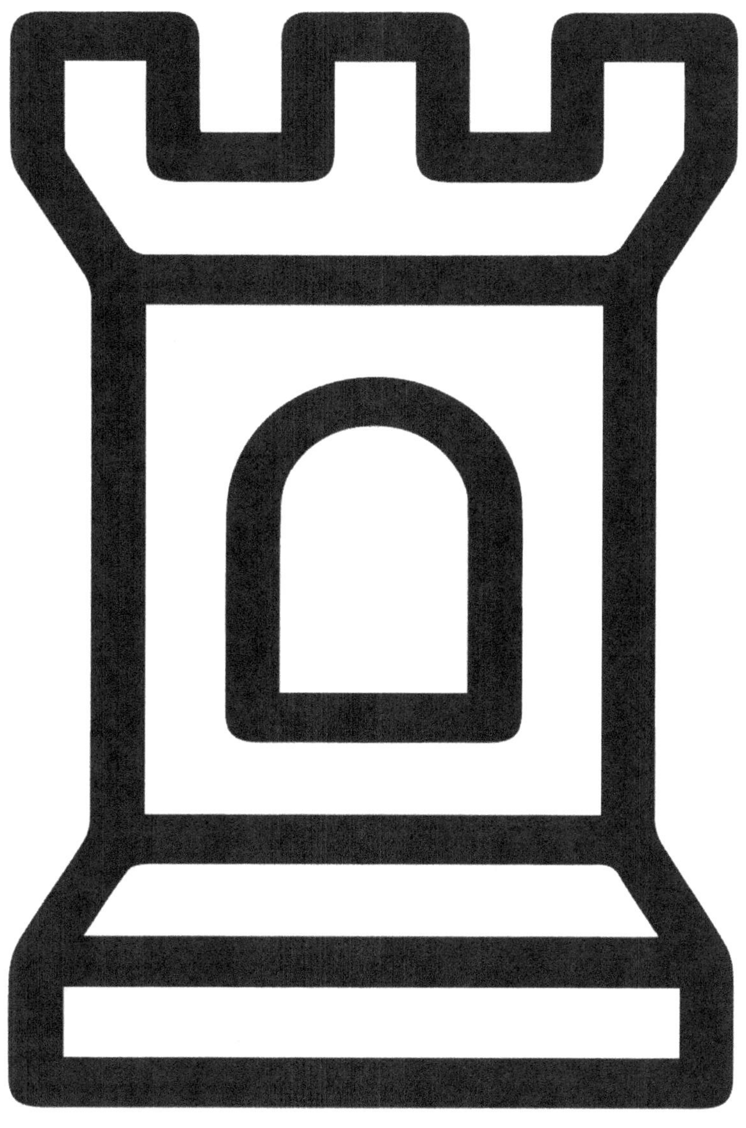

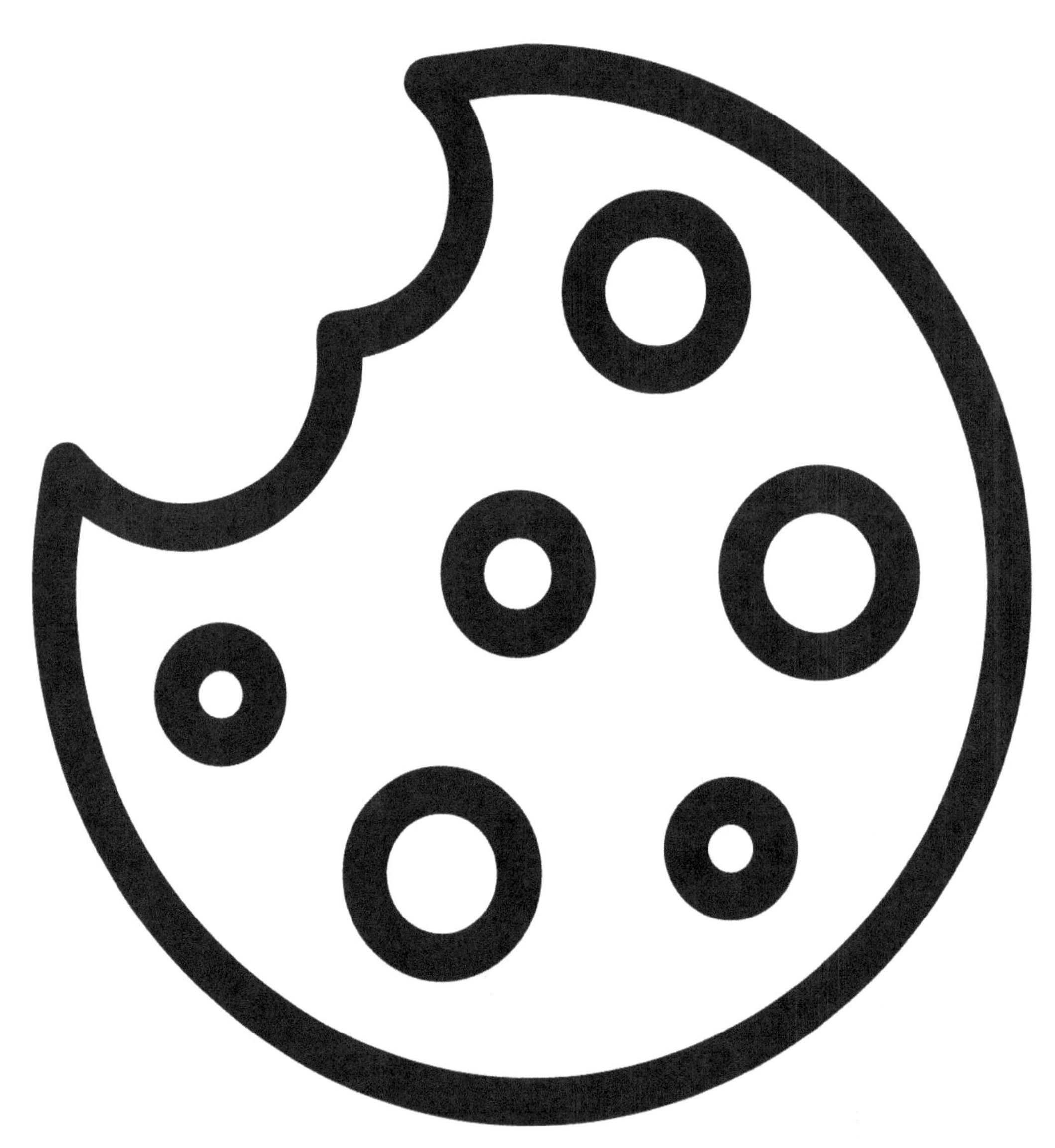

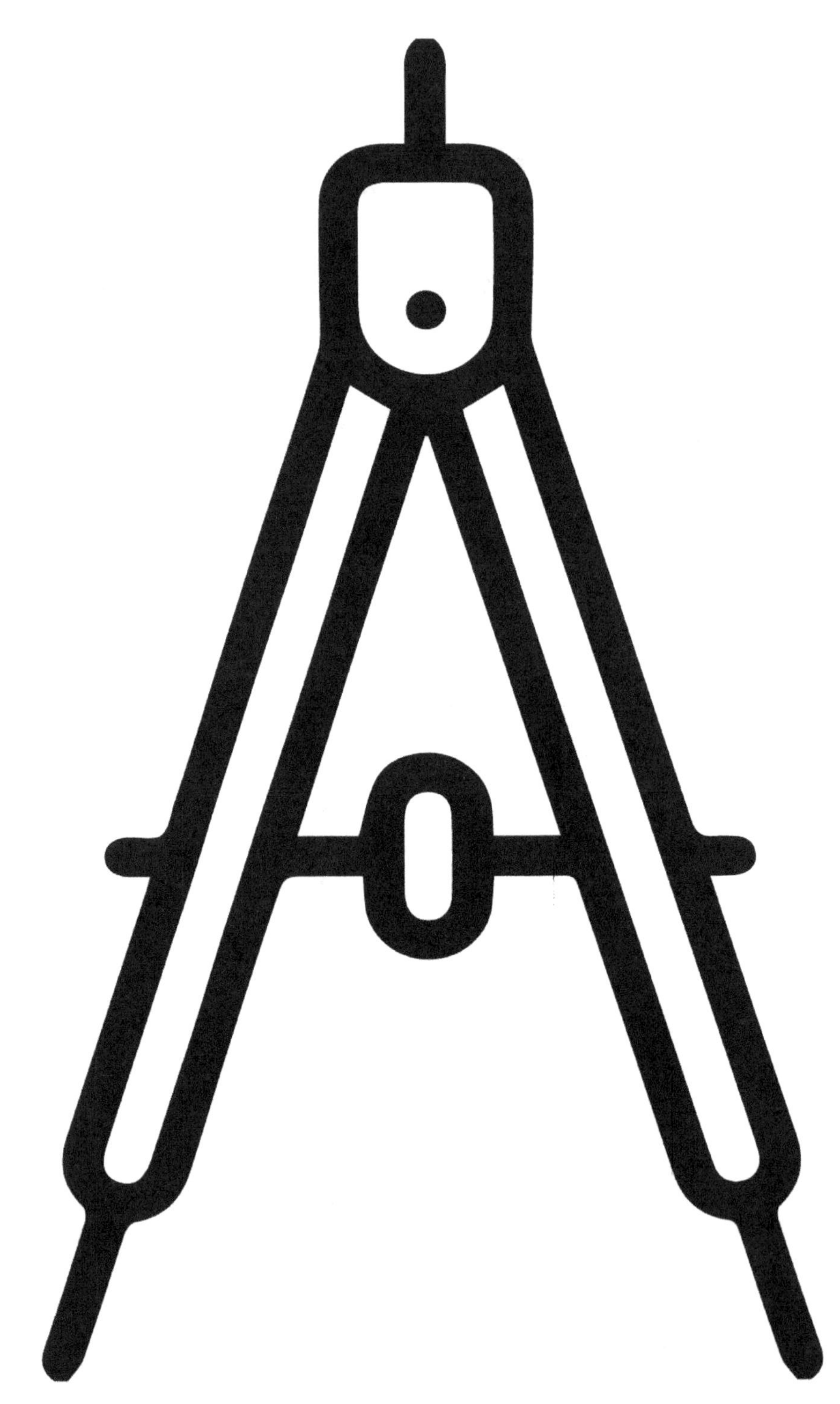

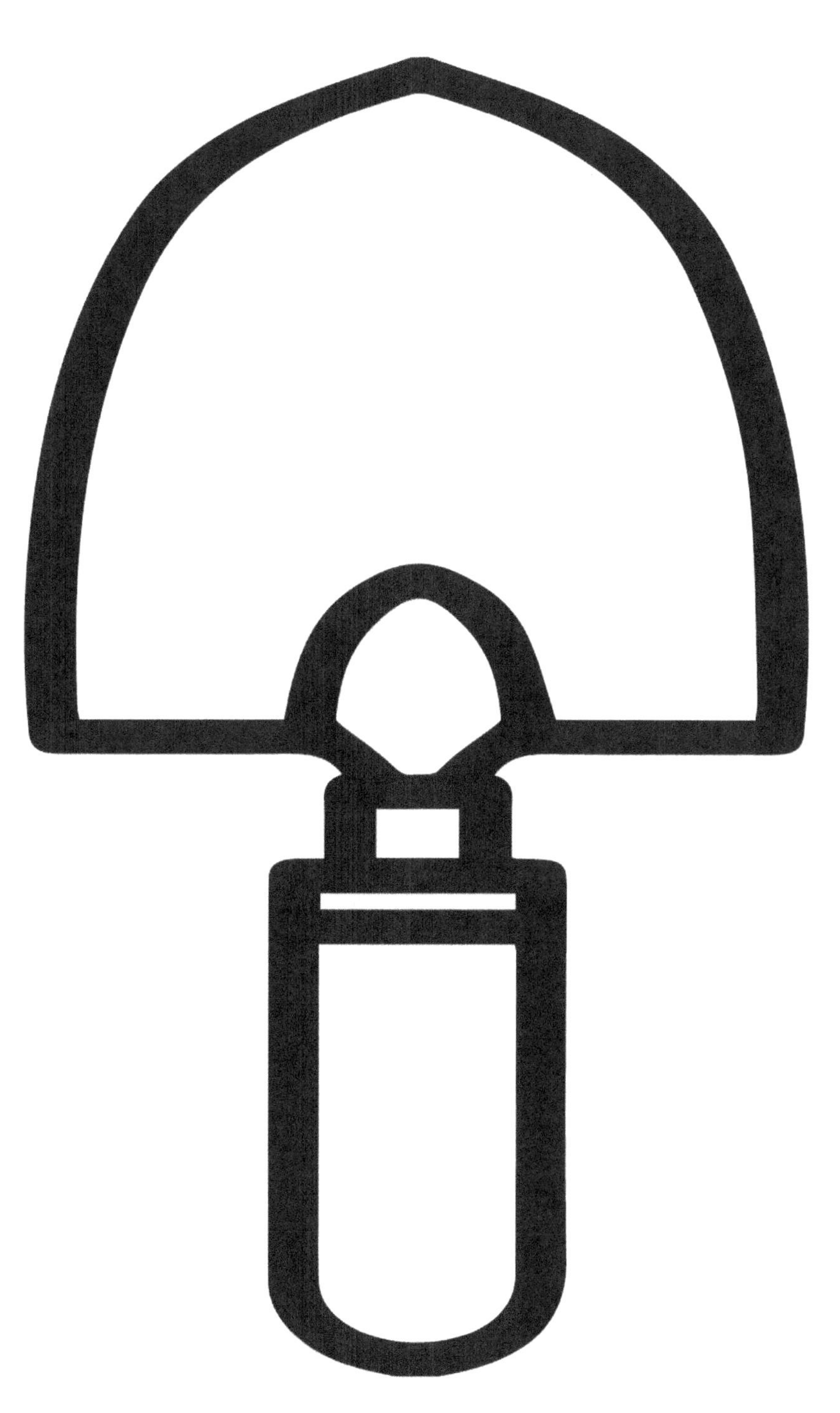

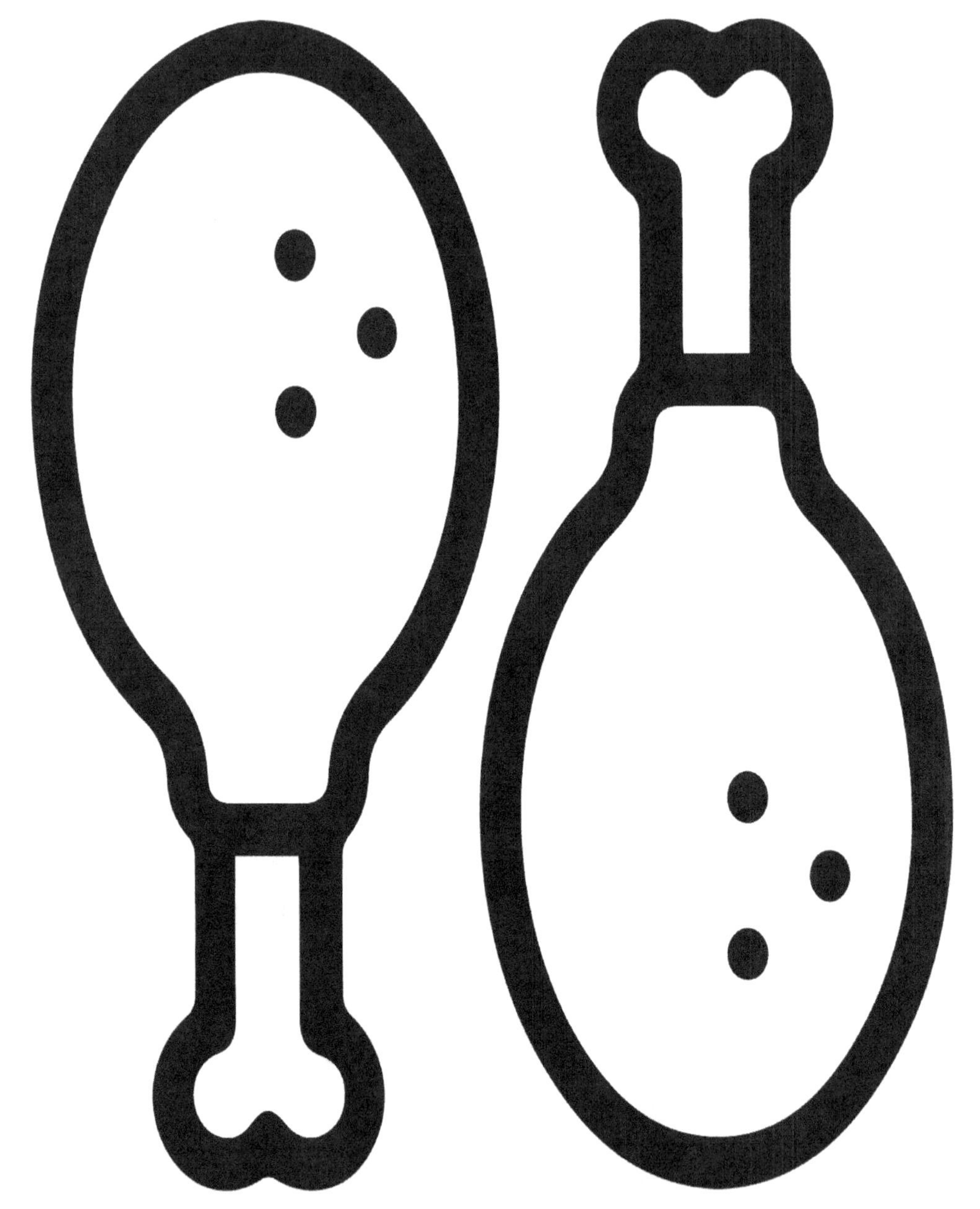

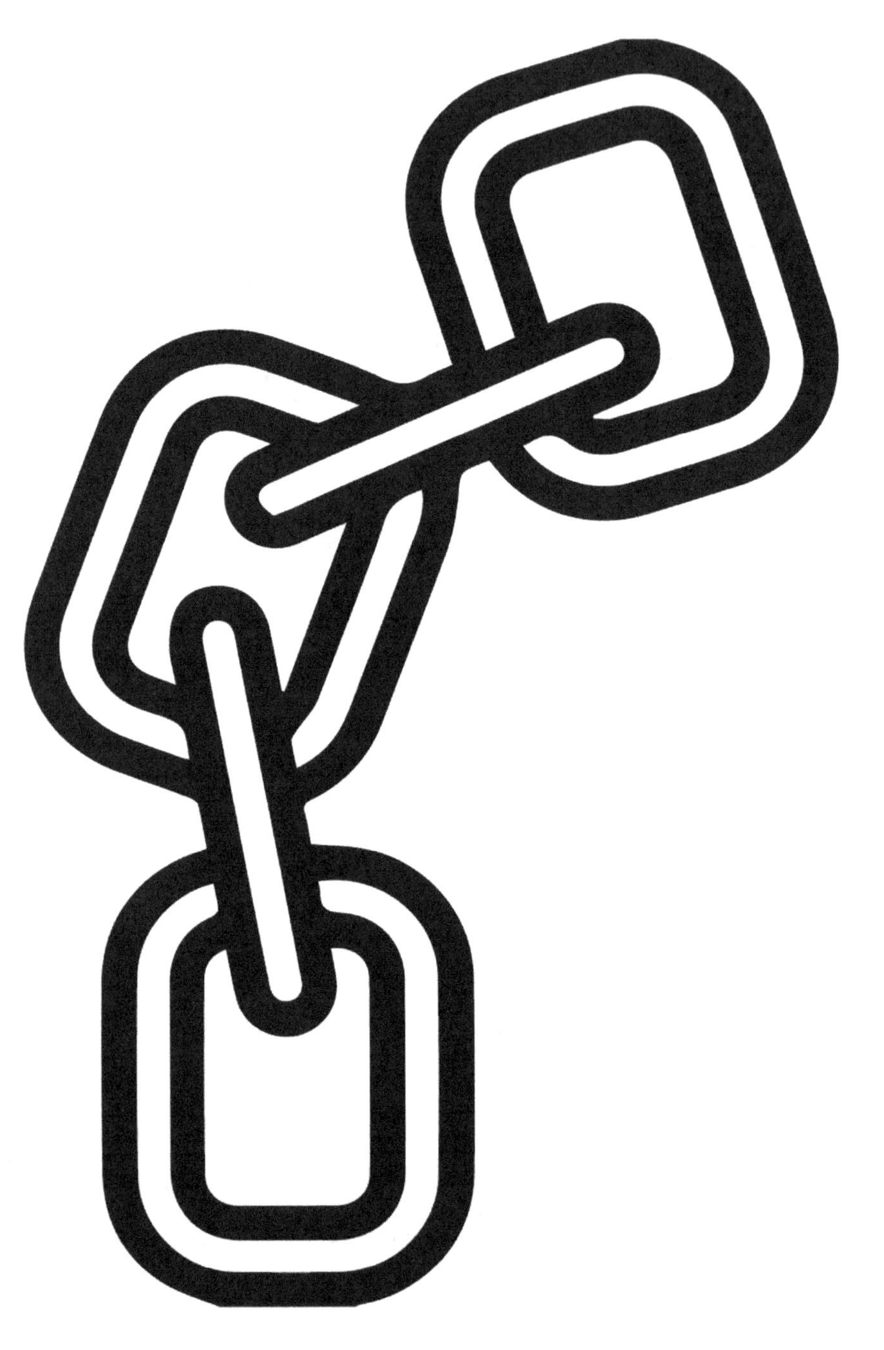

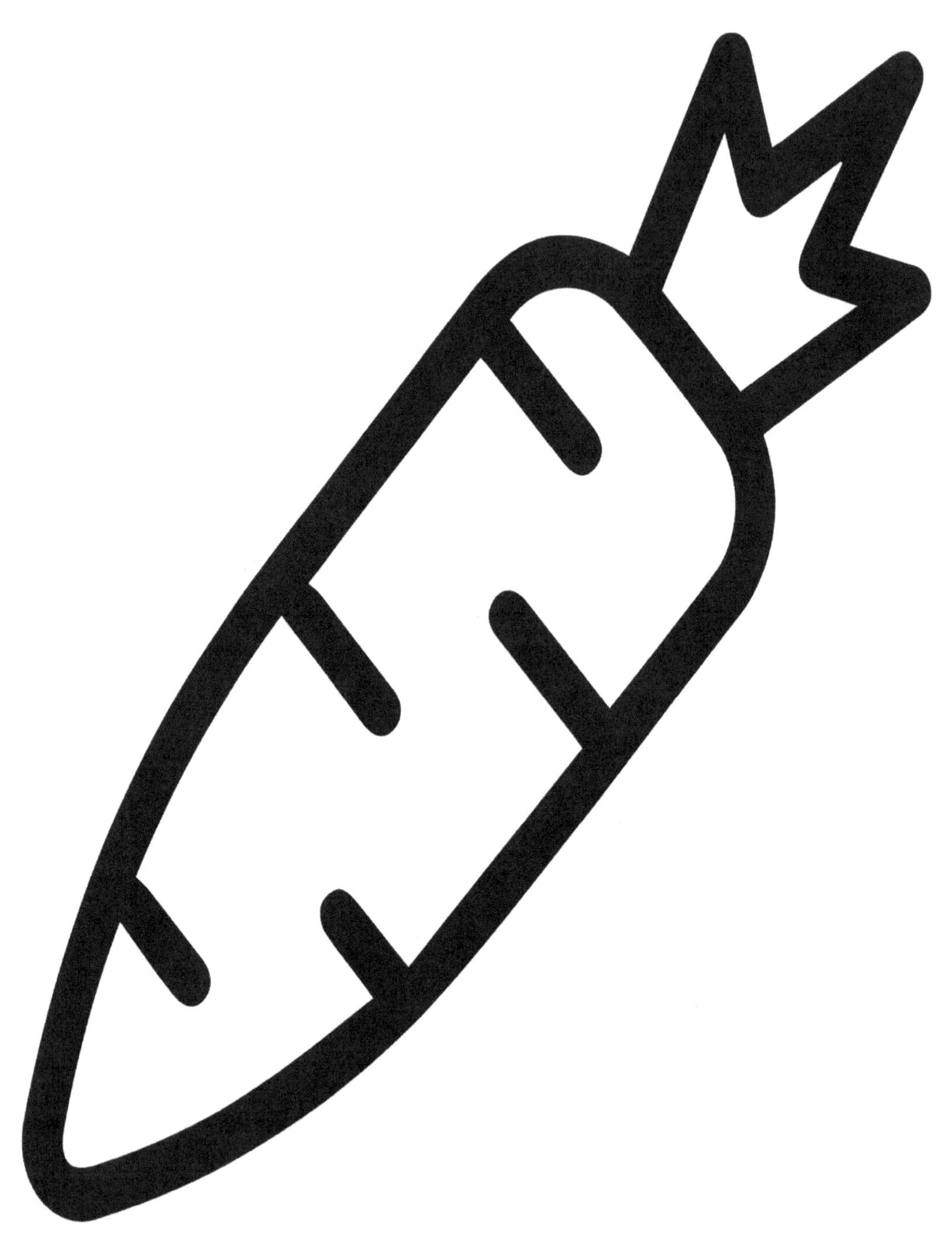

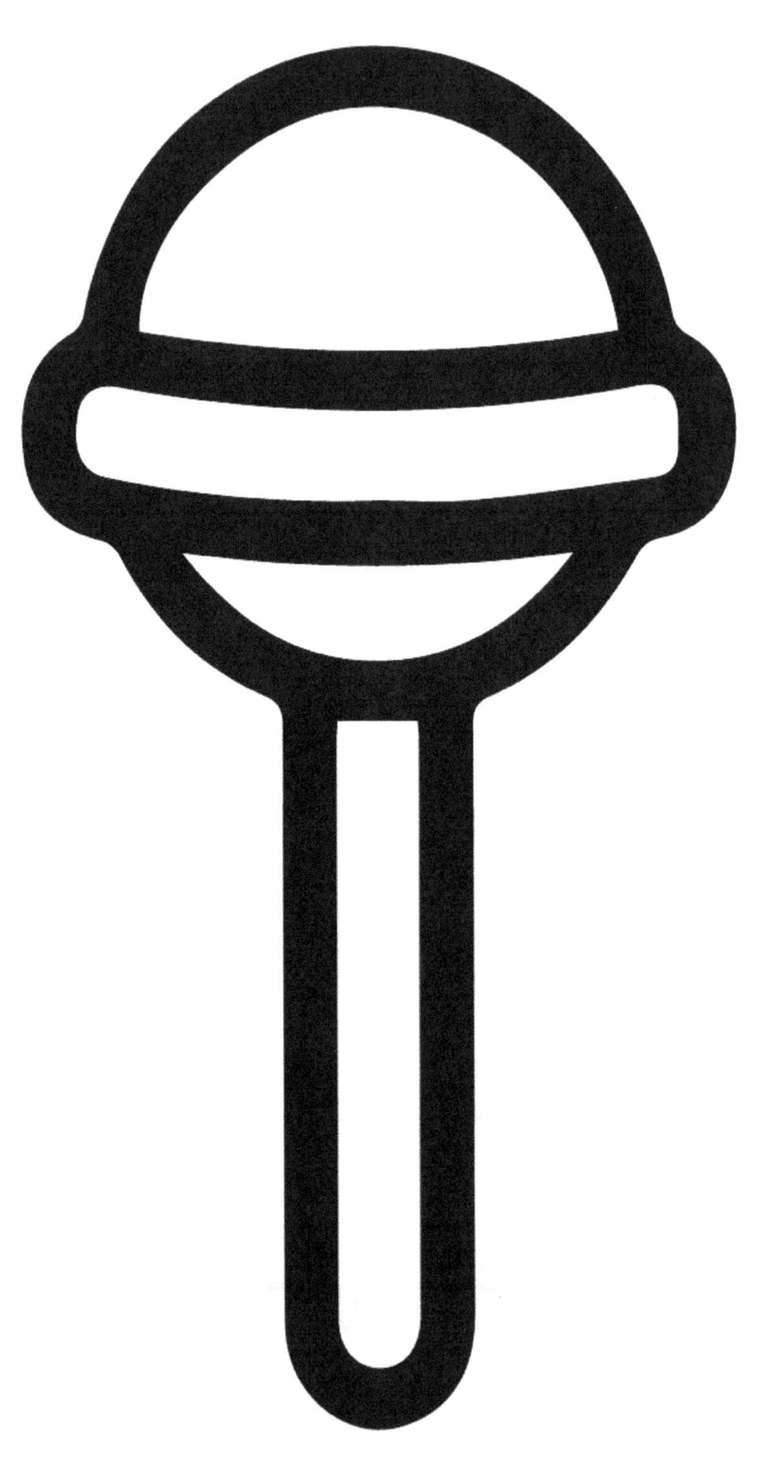

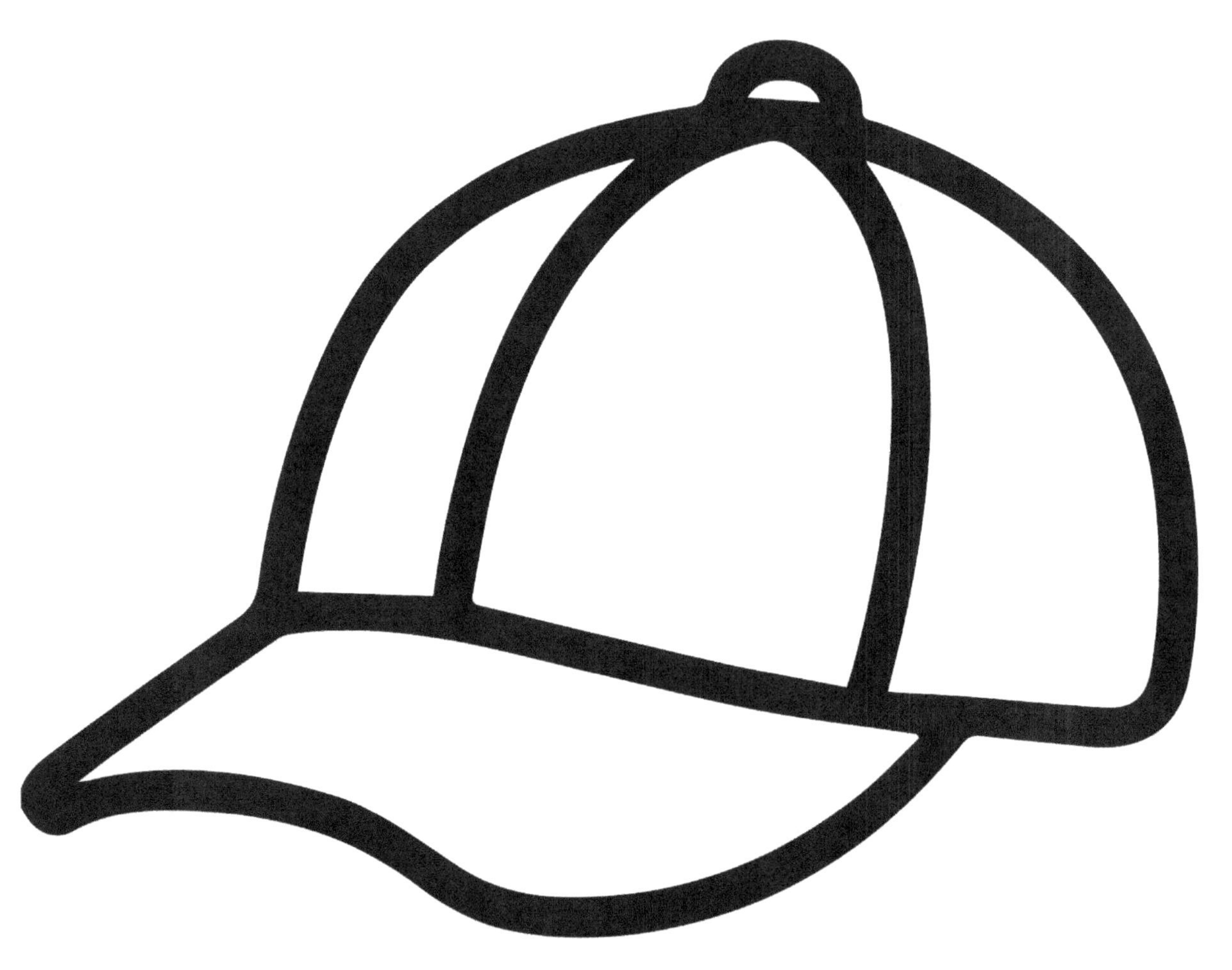

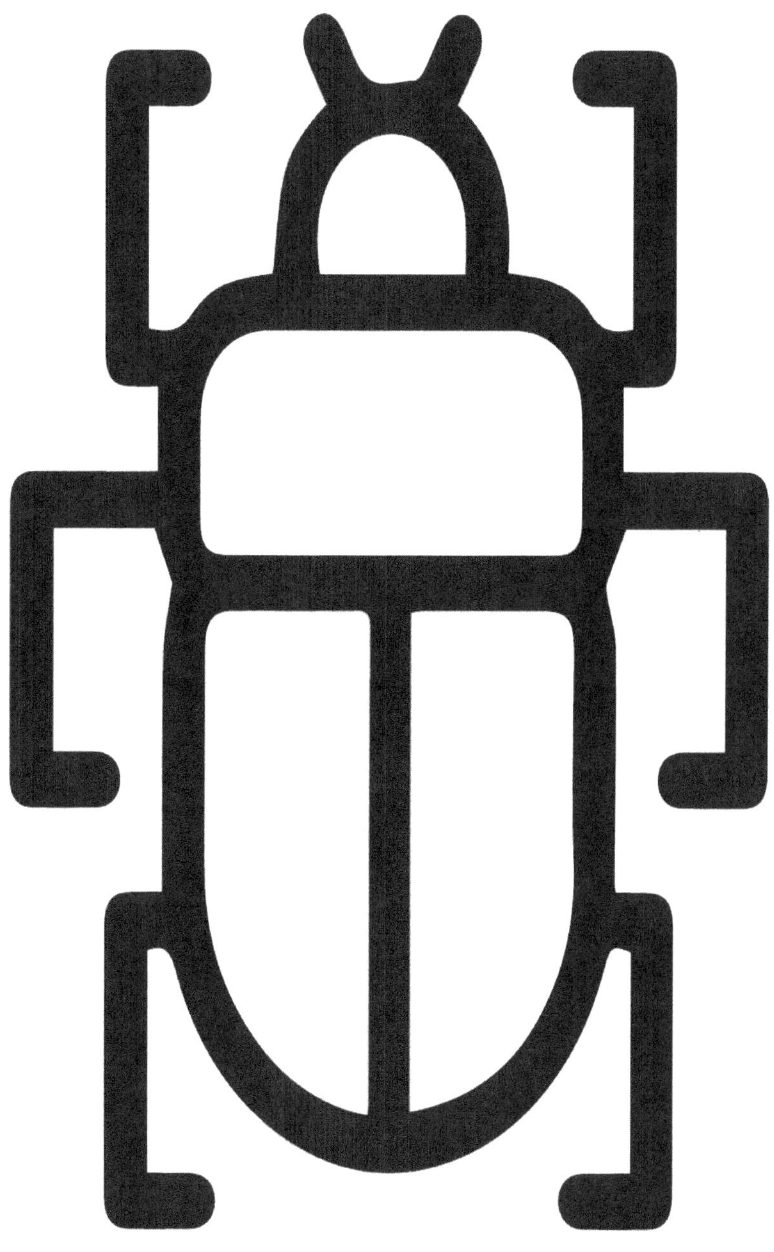

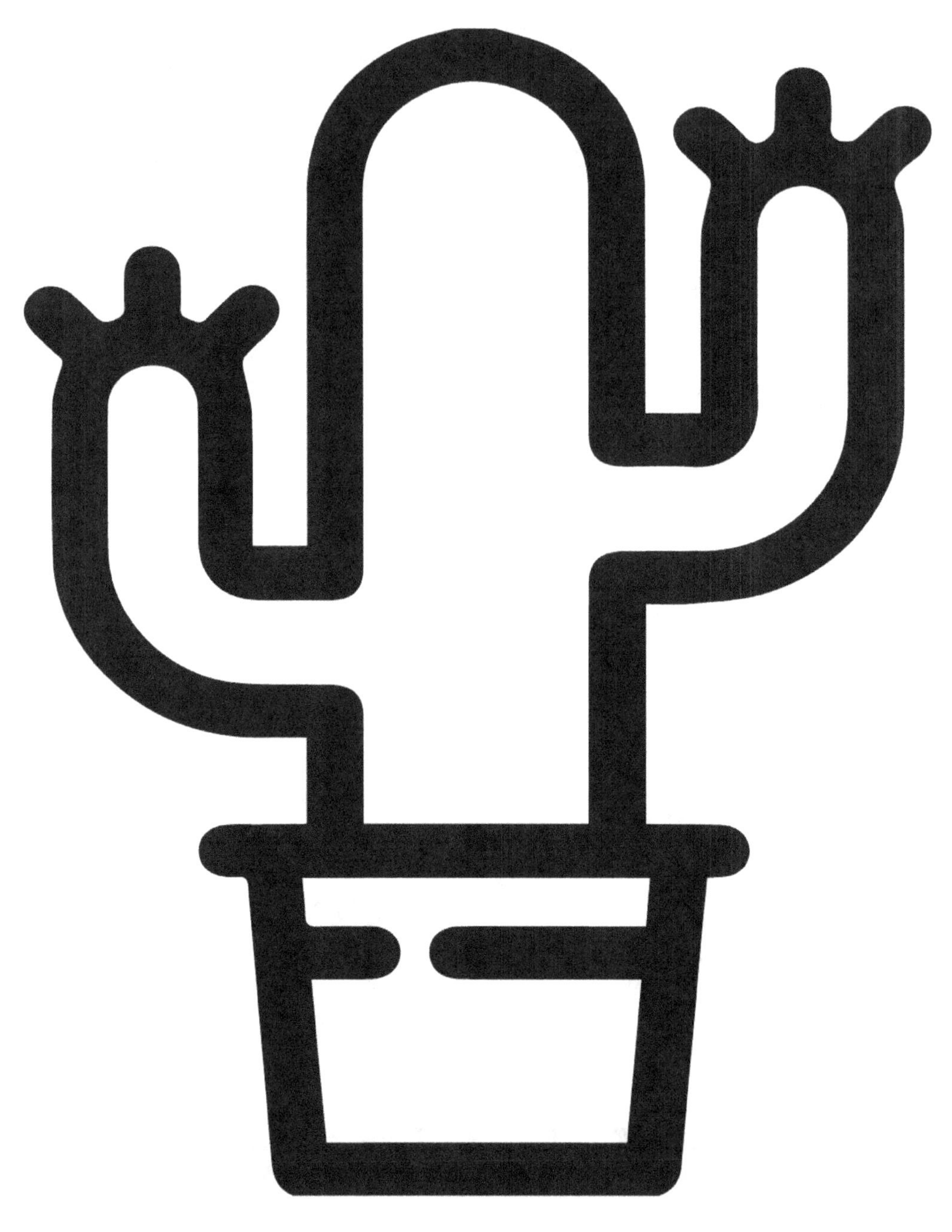

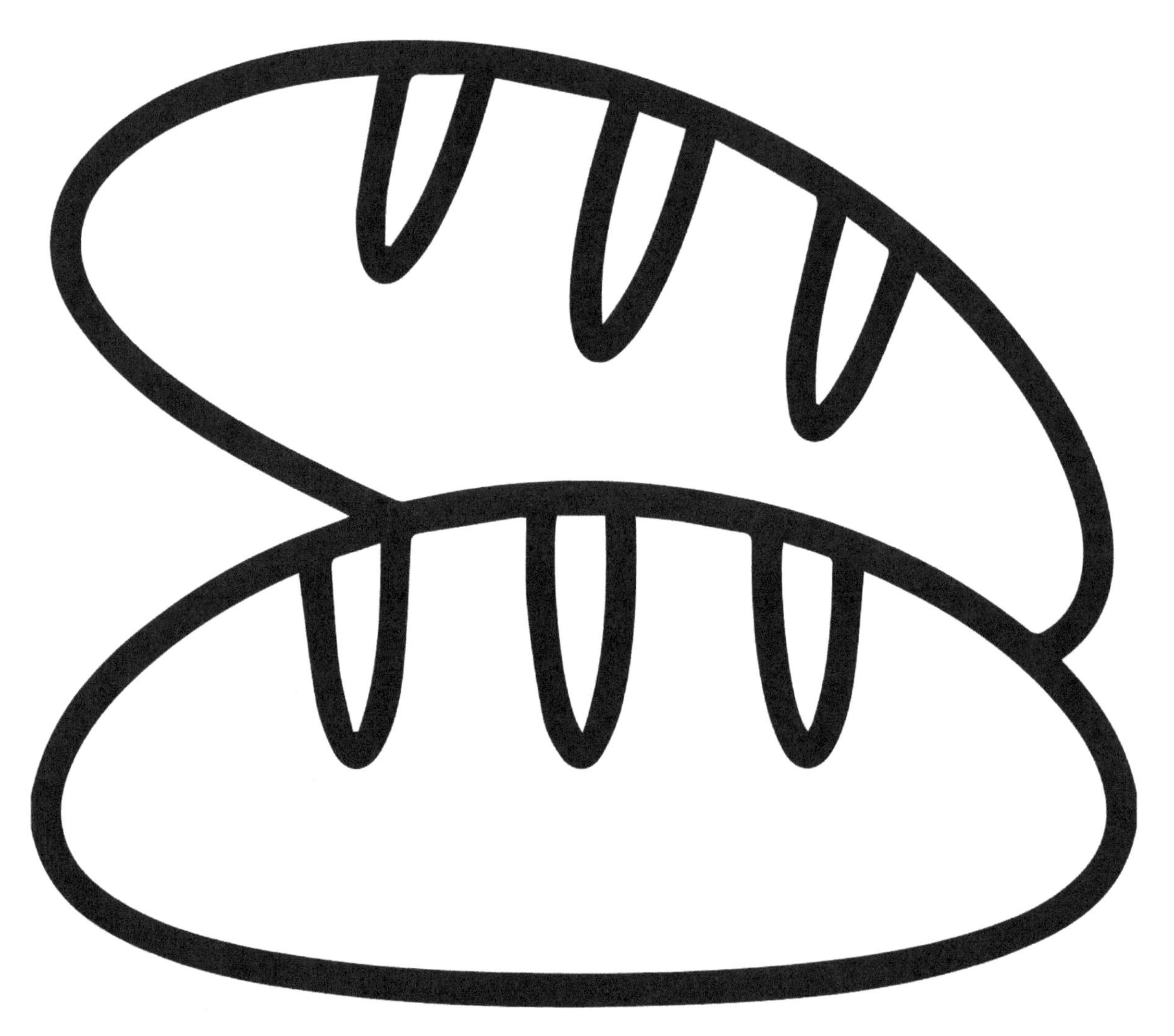

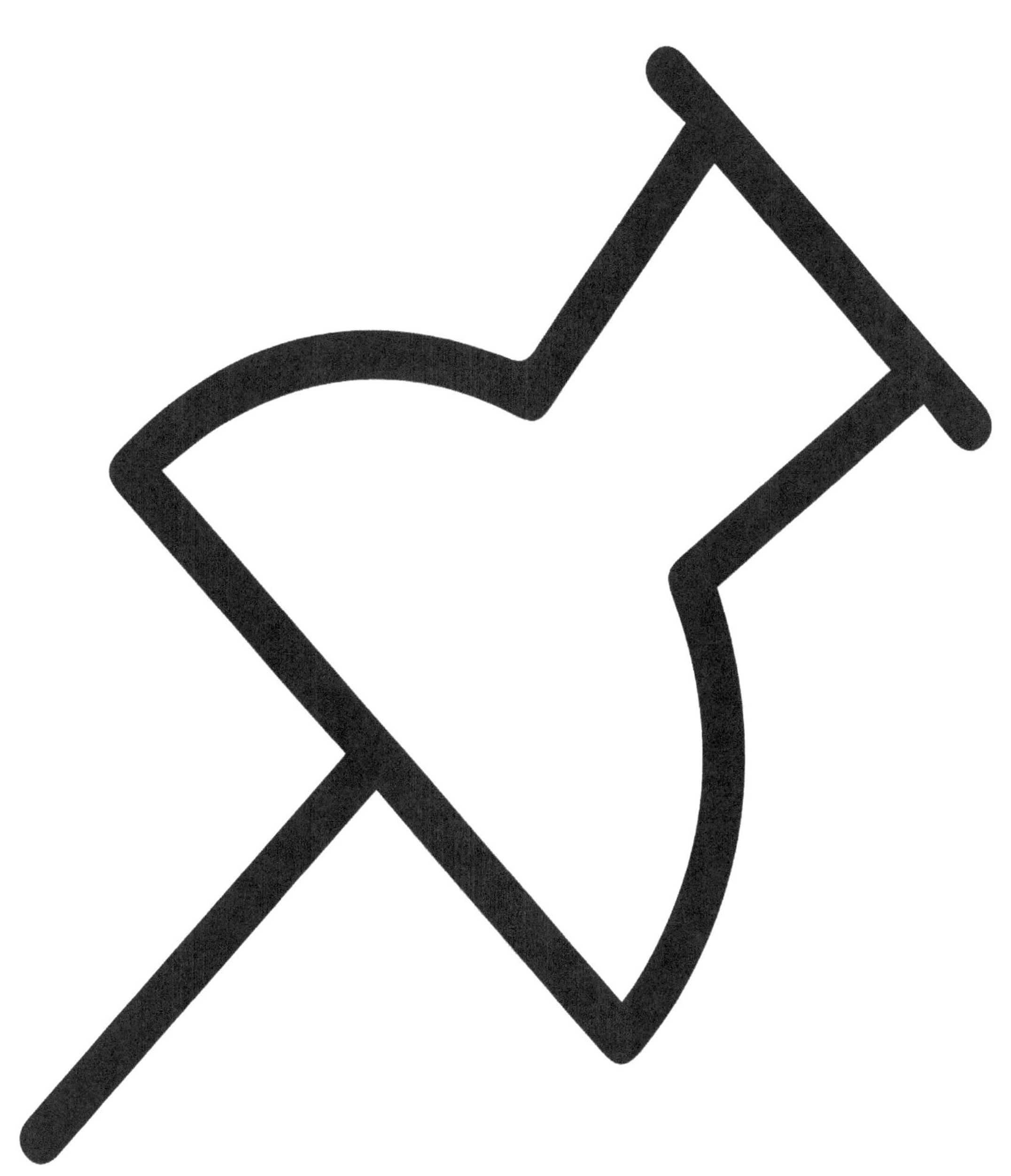

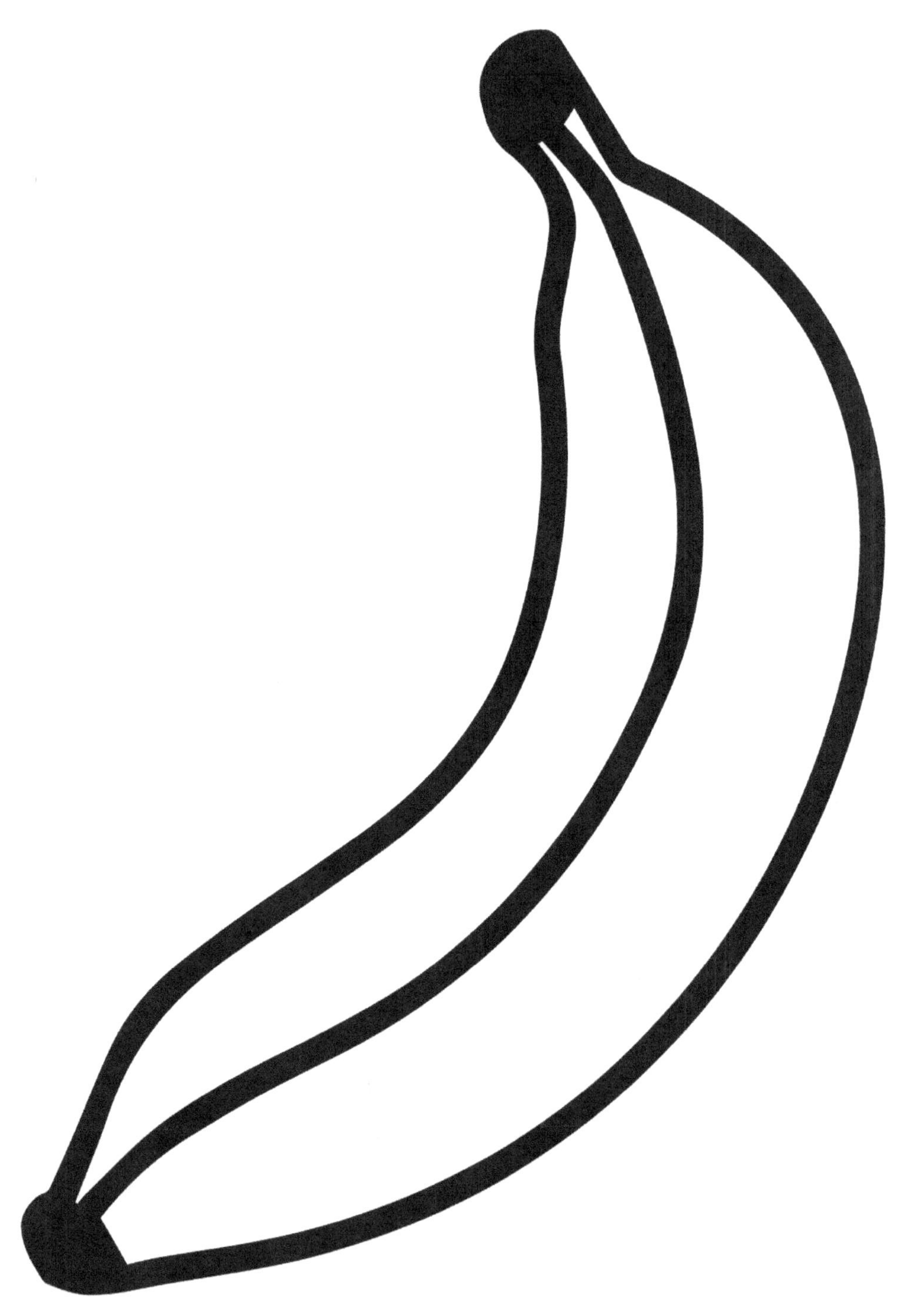

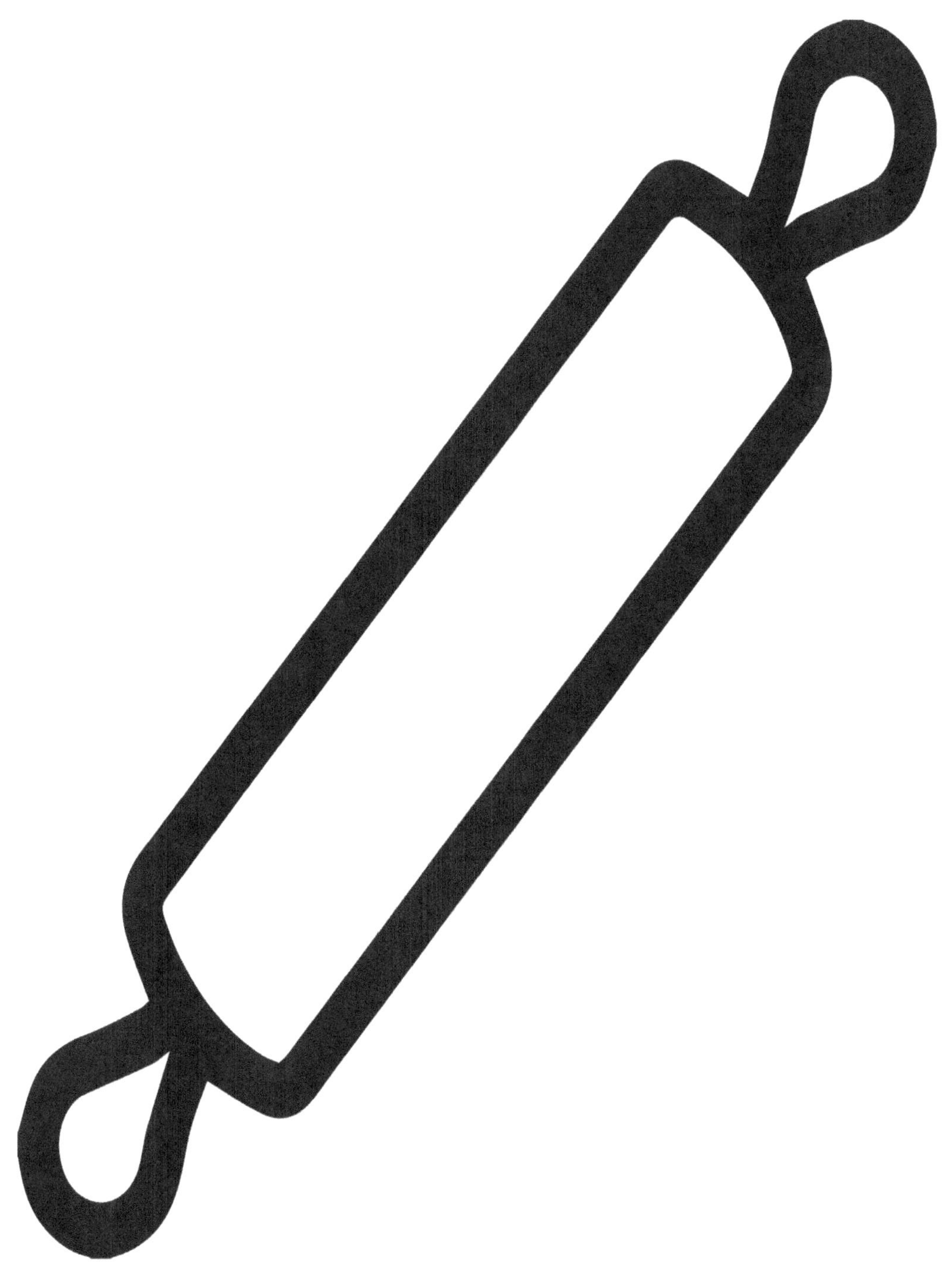